Anonymous

The Origin and Authentic Narrative of the Present Maratta War

Anonymous

The Origin and Authentic Narrative of the Present Maratta War

ISBN/EAN: 9783744678957

Printed in Europe, USA, Canada, Australia, Japan

Cover: Foto ©ninafisch / pixelio.de

More available books at **www.hansebooks.com**

THE ORIGIN

AND

AUTHENTIC NARRATIVE

OF THE PRESENT

MARRATTA WAR;

AND ALSO,

THE LATE ROHILLA WAR,

IN

1773 AND 1774;

Whereby the EAST-INDIA COMPANY's Troops (as Mercenaries) exterminated that brave Nation, and openly drove them for Asylum and Existence into the Dominions of their former most inveterate Enemies.

TO WHICH IS ADDED,

THE UNACCOUNTABLE PROCEEDINGS

IN THE

MILITARY STORE-KEEPER'S OFFICE, in BENGAL.

LONDON:

PRINTED FOR J. ALMON and J. DEBRETT, OPPOSITE BURLINGTON HOUSE, PICCADILLY.

MDCCLXXXI.

PREFACE.

THE title of this small performance, will suffice to announce its contents; the sole purpose of publishing it being, to remove the unjust impression and prejudice which false representations of facts and circumstances have left upon the minds of many persons interested in the event.

HISTORY

OF THE

MARRATTA WAR.

THE Marratta States in the Deccan, are the only people of Hindoſtan who were not effectually ſubdued, or who did not unanimouſly ſubmit to the government, and acknowledge allegiance as fiefs, to the throne of Delhi. They are, conſequently, the only nation of note now exiſting under the dominion of the Hindoo princes. The provinces, or kingdoms of Hindoſtan, were originally governed by princes, who were diſtinguiſhed according to eminence and family, under the titles of *Sou*, or *Ram-rajah*, *Ranah*, and *Rajah*.* The bold and brave efforts of reſiſtance and perſeverance of theſe people, within natural faſteſſes and inacceſſible mountains, which, in a manner preſerved them from bearing the Mogul yoke, may alſo be aſſigned, with a degree of juſtice and propriety, as the true cauſe of their marrauding diſpoſition ſince, a continued neglect of induſtry and agriculture, and an invincible love of arms. While, at the ſame time, they continue to preſerve many of thoſe elevated cuſtoms, and obſerve with ſacred and even ſuperſtitious ſcruples, the laws of hoſpitality in the moſt expanded ſenſe, towards ſtrangers and each other, which, in former times, ſo eminently characteriſed the civilization, addreſs, police, elegance, and virtue of Eaſtern nations.

It

---

* Leſſer characters were known by the names of Paiſhwa, Sardar, Zemindar, Polygar, &c. by the Hindoos. The titles of Viſier, Soubah, Nizam, Nabob, Omrah, &c. accompanied the Mogul government, and continue in the occupation of Mahomedans only.

It is with them, as in all other countries, that by breaking a principal link of the chain, which united a number of diſtinct bodies, the maſs is thrown into anarchy and confuſion, the union is diſſolved, the compact (which rendered them, as one body, great and powerful) is annihilated, and each of the component parts aſſumes the prerogatives of an independent ſovereignty. Hence jealouſies, envy, diſcords, uſurpations, and petty ſtates ariſe, without form, power, or influence.

Amidſt theſe foreign and inteſtine ſtruggles, the Marrattas continued to yield a tacit kind of allegiance to a ſupreme head, as *Sou*, or *Ram-rajah*, whoſe throne was eſtabliſhed at Setterah. The united power of the chief, and his nominal dependants, were extremely great, and often alarming to the Emperors of Hindoſtan. In the time of Aliverdi-Cawn's uſurped Soubahſhip of Bengal, they over-ran thoſe provinces, having, through mere dread, obtained the conſent of the puſilanimous, indolent, and effeminate Mahomed Scha, to eſtabliſh a chout* or tribute to be paid annually from the Nabobſhip of Bengal, and indeed from the whole empire; in the ſame manner as the great Aurungzebe found it prudent, by compoſition, to inveſt them in the Deccan. They marked the terror of their arms and depredations into the heart of Delhi, and carried off vaſt treaſures; until, by the ceſſion of Catac, in the kingdom of Orixa, and a chout of twelve lacks of rupees annually, a peace and treaty were concluded between Aliverdi-Cawn and them, in 1750.

The Marratta revenues, taken disjunctively, were originally enormous. Before the uſurpation and rapid ſucceſs of that ſoldier of fortune, Hyder-Alli-Cawn, in the

---

* *Chout* implies a quarter part of the territorial revenue.

the kingdom of Mysore, and around it, the whole might have bordered upon seventeen crores of rupees, or seventeen millions of British pounds. It is computed, that, now, they enjoy an annual revenue, equal to about twelve millions sterling. Their military establishment, which is composed of cavalry, may yet be equal to 300,000; but these are not to be regarded as regulars, or permanent troops, but as an established militia. The Sou, or Ram-rajah, by virtue of the treaty with Aurengzebe, and by the Hindoo tenures, has power to order out the troops of his tributaries, as often as the state requires their service. It is a circumstance material to be understood, in judging of the Marratta force, that it is an invariable custom among them, when an expedition is concluded, for the troops to retire with what plunder they may have seized, to their respective abodes, leaving only the household forces with the chiefs. And when their services are again wanted, they are summoned by letters, directed to the chief officer of each village, or district, so that they are re-assembled in a week or ten days. The Marratta territory may properly be said to extend, sea-ward, from Travancore near Cape Comorin, at the southern extremity of the peninsula, to the river Paddar, which discharges itself in the Gulf of Scindy, and which divides Guzzerat from the Persian dominions, except the Marratta territory lately usurped by Hyder-Alli-Cawn. They are bounded by the Carnatic, the Company's northern Circars, and the dominions of the Nizam-ul-Muluck,* to the East, except the province of Catac, which carries their possessions, irregularly, to the Bay of Bengal; and the river Jumna, with the provinces of the Mogul empire, terminate their boundary to the North.

The

---

* The Soubah of the Deccan-Bazalet-Jung.

The Sou, or Ram-rajah, exists now but in name. Nana-row, father of the late Mada-row and Narain-row, and brother to the present Roganaut-row, (commonly known by the name of *Ragoba*) seized the reins of government, and the person of the Ram-rajah, at the same instant. The revolution was favoured by the religious Brahmin cast of the usurper. The government he administered under the title of *Paishwa*, or Prime Minister, and the prince he confined in a fortress near Setterah, the metropolis. In this position, the present young Ram-rajah, and the government of the Marratta state, continue to this day. Jonogee Boosla, or Bouncello, the father, or immediate predecessor,* of Moodajee Boosla, Rajah of Berar, was a pretender to the sovereignty, as one of the nearest of kin to the confined Ram-rajah. And Roganaut-row was a pretender to the Paishwa-ship, even during the life-time of his nephew Mada-row, for which Mada-row kept him under confinement, until, foreseeing his own approaching dissolution, and dreading the crafty intriguing disposition of the uncle, even in confinement, to the prejudice of the lineal successor Narain-row, whose youth and inexperience might expose him to snares and plots, thought it most advisable to release Roganaut-row, and effect a reconciliation. Accordingly, having, to all appearances, settled measures, and removed uneasinesses, he placed the hands of the youth into those of the uncle, and shedding tears of joy and satisfaction, said, That he intrusted and recommended the young man, and earnestly besought the uncle's tender care, protection, and advice to him, in the administration of government. A promise which Roganaut-row observed no longer than, by his wiles, he could procure assassins, who cut the nephew to pieces, in the false arms of an uncle,

---

* The right of Moodajee Boosla, in his own person, to the Rajaship of Berar, has lately been challenged by his best friend, Mr. Hastings.

uncle, who thus had no competitor remaining in his own family to the Paiſhwa-ſhip. Mada-row died in November, 1772; and Narain-row was allowed to live until the September following, and the 23d year of his age.

The death of Narain-row being lamented, and the unnatural manner execrated by the generality of people, Roganaut-row's ſucceſſion was oppoſed powerfully. Diviſions became formidable. At laſt the oppoſition prevailed, and the barbarous parricide, Roganaut-row, was obliged to fly. Unhappily, he directed his courſe to the iſland of Bombay, where protection was granted him, in conſideration of a promiſe of flattering conceſſions, which he had neither the power nor right to perform.

The aſylum thus accorded to Roganaut-row, very juſtly incenſed the Marrattas on the one hand, while, on the other, it amuſed with a proſpect of valuable conceſſions of territory, together with the uſual ſpoils and ſuperb acknowledgments which Indian revolutions preſented to the ambitious views of ſucceſsful allies, inſtigated both ſides to commence hoſtilities, apparently with mutual good-will, and ſtimulated appetites.

The marine of Bombay bravely ſuſtained the troops in reducing the iſland of Salſette, after conſiderable loſs to the aſſailants; while the reduction of Baroach coſt the life of one of the beſt and braveſt officers that belonged to either the Britiſh army or the Company's ſervice, in the death of General Wedderburne. The Company felt the loſs ſoon thereafter, by the defeat of the Bombay army under Colonel Keating. Happily, however, by means of the eſtabliſhed enmity between the Marrattas and Hyder-Alli-Cawn, ſeveral jealouſies and heart-burnings between the principal and leſſer ſtates, and diviſions in the Poonah Council, the Marratta government

vernment was, at this time, so divided, that they shewed a serious disposition to preserve the friendship and alliance of the Company, in preference to all other connections; provided the murderer, Roganaut-row, was not supported by them, in an unjust claim, to fully and contaminate the Company's reputation and fame, by a conduct diametrically opposite to the generally received opinion, which, until of late, had been uniformly entertained of the British nation in India.

Had the government of the Company in India the discernment common even to inferior politicians, they would rather have encouraged those enmities, jealousies, and intestine divisions, than by a series of ambitious and mercenary plans and usurpations, and a support of bad characters in iniquitous pretensions, to compel the contending powers, and jarring parties, to unite in the general defence of each other, and their rights, as a common cause.

In this plight were the Company involved with the Marratta state, when the new government, composed of Mr. Hastings, General Clavering, Colonel Monson, Mr. Barwell, and Mr. Francis, commenced, in October, 1774. The newly-arrived members (General Clavering, Colonel Monson, and Mr. Francis) entered upon the duty assigned to them by their country and the Company with alacrity, with sentiments strongly impregnated with true patriotism and justice, and with views solely directed to the recovery of the Company's affairs from the state of embarrassed confusion, debt, and discredit, into which the preceding mal-administration of their principal servants had undutifully plunged them. After selecting the most intelligent and meritorious servants, to administer in the subordinate stations of government, they severely reprehended the Rohilla war, as barbarous, unjust, and impolitic; reprobated,

in

in plain and direct terms, the treaty with Sujah-ul-dowla, and improved upon it with princely advantages in the line of finance and military establishment, in favour of the Company. The spirit of humanity, justice, and œconomy, breathing in every articulation and action, which this uncorrupted majority uttered and performed; they availed themselves of the extended superiority which the act of parliament gave them in certain cases, over the other Presidencies, and sent Colonel Upton upon an embassy, to negociate an honourable peace with the Marratta court; which was at length concluded and ratified, upon the first of March, 1776, under the title of the Poorunder, and sometimes the Poonah, treaty.

By this treaty, Salsette, Baroach, and other districts in the Guzzerat provinces, were ceded to the Company; they were to be paid twelve lacks of rupees in three fixed terms, to defray the charges of the war, to secure which several pergunnahs were delivered up in mortgage possession; and an extent of territory, of the annual value of three lacks, adjoining, or near to Baroach. And, on the other hand, Roganaut-row was to be provided for, according to his rank and pretensions, in a private line, and to withdraw from Bombay; and that no protection or assistance was to be given to him, or any other subject or servant of the Marratta state, who may cause any disturbance or rebellion in the country.

Whether the conditions in this treaty were observed by the contracting parties, whether the proper methods were used for carrying them into execution, or for avoiding a war, or whether the laws of good faith, justice, and policy, were observed in the supreme British Council of India, and the Presidency of Bombay, will appear in the following ingenuous and authentic state

of

of facts, abstracted from uncontested records. Certain, however, it is, that the evil originated in the non-performance of that treaty, and the extraordinary proceedings thereon; that the Marratta government shewed every possible disposition to preserve the friendship, and to maintain an alliance with the English; that a breach of public faith, and an insatiable thirst for power and unbounded monarchy, so apparent in every measure of the Company's servants, united the discordant Marratta states, and jarring members of the administration in Poonah, Hyder-Alli-Cawn, the Soubah of the Deccan, the Rajah of Berar, Nudjiff-Cawn, and all the lesser powers of India, into a combined, determined compact, and close association, to resist, oppose, and reduce the extravagant views and pretensions of the Company's leading administration in Asia; that, urged by the same dread, the native powers, in desperation, discovered inclinations to hearken to the overtures of France, looking wishfully and anxiously with impatience, for the day of deliverance from the scourge of tyranny, and the iron hand of oppression; that these facts have, it is said, been known to the Court of Directors, and to the King's ministers, by the possession of authentic materials; that, by this rash, dishonourable, and unwarrantable war, the Company have had their treasures wasted, their credit ruined, and their reputation for arms almost irretrievably lost; that the Marrattas distinguished more temper, moderation, and good faith, throughout this unlucky business, particularly when victory gave them a *carte-blanche*, than could have been expected from a people of a more pacific disposition, and to whom the opposite qualities are ascribed characteristically. And that it is too evident, from appearances, however artfully disguised, that a train of disgraceful and distressing events, were original objects of the acting administration from the beginning, influenced by sinister views, founded upon ambition,

by

by unabating keen resentment for imaginary preferences, and by an implacable, unremitting opposition to every measure of the majority in the life-time of General Clavering and Colonel Monson, particularly the treaty of Poonah, which they were bent upon overturning, at all hazards. There are reasons to imagine, that it was proposed to derive some oblique justification of the Rohilla war, from the unfavourable effects of an ill-conducted Marratta war.

Roganaut-row, under the protection of the Bombay government, entered into intrigues, and fomented parties and dissentions in the administration of Poonah, until at length, he procured an infatuated deception upon the simple credulity of the unsuspecting Resident, Mr. Mostyn, who in consequence of his own easy faith, as easily misled the willing minds of the Presidency of Bombay into a belief of what they so eagerly wished.

The Governor General, Mr. Hastings, introduced the subject at the supreme board, upon the 28th day of January 1778, in a very long minute, wherein, among a variety of other matters, he complained bitterly of the silence and remissness of the Presidency of Bombay, although Mr. Mostyn had had several conferences with the Poonah ministers, who continued to complain that Roganaut-row was still entertained at Bombay, in violation of orders from the supreme board. He added, that new sources of uneasiness had arisen, in the extraordinary countenance afforded to the Chevalier St. Lubin and Mr. Bolts, by the court of Poonah; one as agent to the crown of France, the other as representative of the House of Austria. That if report could be believed, written engagements had passed between them and Monsieur St. Lubin, " *the object of*
" *which, whatever it be, must if attained, prove destruc-*

" *tive to the trade of the English Company, and to the Bri-*
" *tish influence in India.*" *

These being the ideas which Mr. Hastings laboured to impress on the minds of his fellow-counsellors, as an evil which threatened destruction, by the alarming power of the Marrattas—As a wise and faithful servant and subject, would it not have been more consistent, and infinitely more just and political, to have accommodated the breach, and applied a healing balsam to the sore, by an observance of the late treaty, and good faith, than wantonly to urge a dangerous, expensive, and unjust war?

At the same moment, Mr. Hastings acknowledged,
" *that although he believed the Marratta power, unallied*
" *with other states, unable to cope with the Company's*
" *power at Bombay, yet sustained by the French, they are*
" *qualified to refuse acquiescence to our demands; which de-*
" *mands, the possession of the island of Basseen offers, as the*
" *only prospect of a security; that no obligation precludes us*
" *from demanding it, nor can any blame be justly imputed to*
" *us, if as the Superior Power, we prescribe the terms,*
" *were they even more unequal than these are, on which we*
" *are willing to release both parties, from that dangerous*
" *point on which they fluctuated, between war and peace,*
" *during a long interval of two years, and are likely to con-*
" *tinue there, unless one side assumes the right of decision.*"

In

---

* Hyder-Alli having resented the profers of St. Lubin to the Marrattas, and the Marrattas unwilling to irritate the English, no concession or treaty whatsoever was entered into with Mr. St. Lubin, and he was expressly desired to withdraw from Poonah. He had had partizans there who wished to promote his views. He went to Hyder-Alli, and the refusal of the Marratta government contributed to facilitate the treaty, and the cession of the port of Mangalore. This was, and is the fact.

In this paffage of his minute, Mr. Haftings unguardedly avows facts, which in direct terms condemn his own deliberate meafures. The extenfive advantages which a French alliance would yield to the Marrattas, fhould have induced him to treat upon more liberal, equal, and juft principles, as the moft likely means of overfetting the fufpected treaty with St. Lubin. He avows, "*danger to both fides,*" and a confeffion tantamount to its having been a ftudied impending manœuvre in his political fyftem, "*for a long interval of two years,*" which comprehends the intire time that the Poonah treaty had exiftence. According to his profeffed maxims, "*the fword and not juftice, fhould decide the point of right,*" in an iffue in which the Company had, *bona fide*, no concern, and became unneceffarily and imprudently, officious medlers. The great and acknowledged abilities of Mr. Haftings, and particularly the fingular talent which he has acquired in writing, are circumftances which, upon a critical review and examination of his minutes and general conduct, fince his return with power to India, will, upon many occafions, condemn himfelf, even more than the mafterly pens of his opponents. The art of evafion, and equivocation, for the purpofes of veiling or difguifing the real meafures taken, or meant to be taken, are too confpicuous not to create fufpicions of the matters thus meant to be fupported or defended. Plain, inequivocal facts, carry conviction where the ground is really found, and the meafures themfelves directed to wife and falutary purpofes; but when the mind is confcious of having betrayed truft, or is perverfely bent upon, and determined, to guide and enforce meafures, whether right or wrong, by the exercife of power abufed and mifapplied, the faculties of evafion, equivocation, and confequently of perverfion, are employed with dangerous and alarming advantages in the fupreme magiftrate of a remote government, vefted with civil, military,

litary, political, and commercial powers. The arguments and reasonings expressed in the minutes of Mr. Haltings, upon this and other important subjects, since the treaty of Benaras, contain such palpable contradictions to each other, and duplicity of sentiment, as are sufficient, without the able opposition they have had to encounter, to condemn the whole. And the inattention of the Directors to these subjects, regularly transmitted to them, nearly establishes an unpleasant truth, that although charged with a trust of magnitude and dignity, they scarcely ever read the proceedings of their servants, on the most important concerns of the Company and nation, in India.

The Governor proposed a plan, composed of ten articles, as the terms to be asked and insisted upon from the Marrattas, and being opposed by Mr. Francis and Mr. Wheler, the consideration was put off till the day following.

1778, January 29th. On which day, the Governor laid before the Board, a letter from the Presidency of Bombay, concerning the subject of yesterday's complaint. In this letter, dated the 12th December, 1777, they give notice of an offer made by some members of the ministerial party at Poonah, to reinstate Roganaut-row, and of their own determination to accept such offer, whenever it should be authenticated by a direct engagement from the ministers, and to march with Rogaanaut-row, to establish him in the Paishwa-ship of Poonah by force of arms. They condemn the countenance given to Mr. Bolts, as well as to Mr. St. Lubin, and amuse themselves with the greater assurance of success in favour of Roganaut-row, as they expect assistance from Hyder-Alli-Cawn, who professes a friendship for that party; *an advantage which, however, they neglected to improve.* And the Governor reduced the propositions of yesterday

day from ten to five articles, without any material variation in point of matter, to the following purport, *viz.*

I. That such reasonable and practicable security be obtained for the personal safety of Roganaut-row, *as Roganaut-row himself shall require.*

II. That a specific sum be demanded to reimburse the company for the military charge, which may be incurred by that interposition.

III. That the fort and district of Basseen be ceded in perpetuity to the Company.

IV. That an additional grant of territory be made adjacent to Basseen and Bombay, in exchange for Baroach, and the lands ceded by Futta-Sing-Guiacawar, and from the pergunnahs of Hanfood, Aumood, and Desborah.

V. That no European settlement be allowed on any of the maritime coasts of the Marratta dominions, *without the consent of the supreme council previously obtained.*

These demands were sufficiently imperious and dictatorial, to a powerful independant state; but the 9th of the propositions of yesterday, contained a more imperious tone, in these terms: "*That these proposals be conveyed by letter to the present Paishwa; that his answer be required,* without condition or reserve, *to each article; and that this government shall take its final resolution, to abide by the treaty, as it shall stand confirmed by his answer, or to consider it as annulled and invalidated by them.*"

It is worthy of observation, that at a juncture so confessedly critical, notwithstanding the objectionable part of Mr. Bolt's political conduct, recorded on the proceedings

ceedings in Bombay, and the positive injunctions of the Company concerning his object in India, the very leading members of that government, afforded him the most essential assistance in his undertakings, of which the ship Louisa, and her cargoes to and from China, furnished the clearest evidence. And it is somewhat extraordinary, that however impolitic it might prove, to establish the avowed friend and partizan of Hyder-Alli-Cawn, at the head of the Marratta government, yet, as they had determined upon the measure, they should certainly have formed some plan of accommodation, to which Hyder should engage, as a party; although, upon every possible principle of good policy, the Marratta alliance was a more natural and beneficial connection to the Company, and more to be depended upon, than an aspiring, ambitious usurper, whose enmity to the English, and their allies, was as firmly rooted as that which he entertained for the Marrattas. It would therefore have been the essence of good policy, in the Company's servants, to have made use of their influence in preserving the division, and countenancing the jealousies, of two states, whose junction of power, should it ever happen, would effectually crush and destroy all the future prospects of the British nation in Hindostan.

Mr. Francis entered a formal protest against the Bombay proceedings; doubted the sincerity of the conference between Mr. Lewis (the assistant resident at Poonah) and Amunt-row, for the restoration of Roganaut-row; urged the propriety of a steady adherence to the Company's general instructions, and particularly to their reprehensive letter of 12th April, 1775, addressed to the Presidency of Bombay: He wished, he said, to obtain the right and possession of Basseen for the Company, "*by an amicable negociation of exchange, or purchase;*" but declared, "*that even his views were cooled, by the little utility in point of revenue, arising from the conquest of*
Sal-

" *Salsette."* * His reasons throughout are clear, judicious, and predictory of what followed. Mr. Wheler manifested the warmth of zeal and duty, in opposition to the proceedings in Bombay, as having an immediate tendency to consume the Company's revenues, and to involve their means and reputation in distress and ruin. †

Upon the 2d February, 1778, Mr. Hastings's proposals were re-considered; opposed, as before, by Mr. Francis and Mr. Wheler, and carried by the Governor's *casting vote*, to support Roganaut-row, in direct violation of the Poorunder treaty; and, with three additional articles, were ordered to be dispatched to the Presidency of Bombay, for their government.

The Governor then proposed, to take the opinion of General Stibbert on the sending a reinforcement, over the continent to Bombay, and the consequent necessity of augmenting the Sepoy corps: He also proposed a letter to Madras, to induce that Presidency to reinforce the Bombay army from thence; and at the same instant, that he continued with confidence, to assert, " *that the* " *Presidency of Bengal is, and will be, in a condition to* " *assist Bombay abundantly, with men and money, to carry* " *on the Marratta war*," he stated the Bombay army thus:

Artillery, rank and file	261
European infantry	783
Sepoy infantry	5621
Irregulars	1231

A force which he thought able to carry all their hostile purposes into execution, without any assistance from Bengal

---

* It is confidently alledged, that the present clear revenue of Salsette, is far short of the real advantages it yielded in the line of commerce, when it was in the possession of the Marrattas.

† Vide the Company's records, for these minutes.

Bengal or Madras; an opinion which he struggled to enforce, by comparing it with the force of Bengal at the battle of Plassey, and against the Scha Zadda; with Colonel Forde's expedition against Masulipatnam; and considerably greater, than when unsupported by country powers, the troops of Bengal wrested the provinces and Soubaship from Cossim-Alli-Cawn. And thus, he affected to draw the same successful conclusions in the present affair, without considering, that the Marrattas are professionally and constitutionally, a warlike nation; whereas the Bengalee's are the most timid, irresolute, and indolent part of the human species. He might also, have considered that Fortune has proved herself as fickle and inconstant, in the decision of arms, as in the dispensation of other fortuitous events, which affect empires, states, societies, and individuals. He computed the distance from Bombay to Poonah at only four days march; that the friends of Roganaut-row were encamped in the neighbourhood of Poonah with 20,000 horse, and that his opponents, together with the main Marratta army, were engaged hostilely against Hyder-Alli-Cawn on the banks of the Kistna, therefore could not assist against the friends and measures of Roganaut-row.

How unfortunate was Mr. Hastings, as well in his secret intelligence, as in his conjectures, *if they were such as he expressed!* The Bombay army were not within two days march of Poonah, after having been about fifty days in their progress,* without any hostile obstruction, before they were totally defeated, and forced to a disgraceful humiliation, and a *carte-blanche.* There was not a man in the civil or military

admini-

---

* The expedition moved from Bombay on the 22d of November, and after three or four days skirmishing, they capitulated at Wargaum on the 16th of January, distance about twenty-five or thirty miles from Poonah.

administration of the Marratta government, either in thought or action, ready to espouse the cause of Roganaut-row; but, on the contrary, the whole body of the people, in every station, seemed unanimous to oppose him, and the plan and measure he had adopted; and when it came to the test, the Bombay army found so numerous a force to oppose their approaches, that they were surrounded, and hemmed in at all quarters, by such a body of troops, that it proved the Marratta main army were not on the banks of the Kistna. By this rule of judging, are not the following queries directly applicable? Is not the Governor General, by the countenance which he gave, and fallacious representations made by him, by which the Presidency of Bombay were not only encouraged, but justified, and even spirited on, culpable in a greater degree than as an accessary? And is he not immediately and directly answerable, with his fortune and person, to the Company and British nation, for all the treasure and troops which have been lost unnecessarily, and the disrepute and discredit brought on the Company and the nation, by the unwarrantable and wanton manner in which he forced the Company into the Marratta war? — The mode of approbation by the Supreme Council, and the conditions which accompanied it, as requisitions inadmissable by the Marrattas, are material justifications of the Bombay gentlemen, against censures which otherwise should have irretrievably crushed them. Mr. Hastings's inconsistency, or whatever other definition it may admit of, appears in a reply to the eighth paragraph of Mr. Francis's minute. He proposed, "*to enter into a* "*war with the most powerful state in Hindostan, who* "*he conjectured were in alliance with Fraance, as the* "*means of defeating the views of France and Spain.*" Instead of endeavouring to make that "*most powerful* "*state,*" forsake the alliance of France, and become the faithful friends and allies of the British nation,

C and

and thus render the Company's poffeffions fo fecure, that the whole power and force of Britain might be directed elfewhere, with effect, againft its enemies.— The Marrattas offered to fettle a jaghire of five lacks of rupees annually on Roganaut-row, provided he would withdraw to Benaras, under the Englifh protection. This Mr. Haftings oppofed, and by that means, refufed peace and fecurity, together with the reception of about £.60,000 fterling annually, in fpecie, from a country with which the Company have no mercantile intercourfe from Bengal or Bahar.

The 9th of February, Mr. Haftings informed the Board, that by private intelligence, he had received affurance of Governor Bellecombe's departure from Pondichery to the Malabar Coaft, with a defign to receive folemn poffeffion of the port of Choul, on the part of France, in confequence of a ceffion thereof by the Marrattas. The truth was, that Monf. Bellecombe made a tour to Mahe in the Brilliante man of war, and doubtlefs had in view, to affift Mr. St. Lubin, in forming and concluding treaties with the Marrattas and Hyder-Alli-Cawn. But the port of Choul never had been, either the object of his expedition, nor the probable conceffion on the part of a ftate, already too jealous and fufpicious of European influence and intrigues in their vicinity.

On the 23d of February, Mr. Haftings prefented a letter from Bombay of the 20th January, on which, it would feem, that he founded his motion for marching a detachment over land to re-inforce the Bombay army. Mr. Francis and Mr. Wheler perfifted to oppofe it, and protefted in the ftrongeft terms againft the refolves of the majority.* The Governor's double vote

* Vide the minutes upon record.

vote, and the single one of Mr. Barwell, having overruled the two single votes of their opponents, a detachment under the command of Colonel Matthew Leslie was resolved upon, to consist of

Officers	103
Troops	6,624
Servants	19,729
Bazar people	12,000
	38,456

Here was an army of 6727 troops only, and a suite of 31,729 servants and sutlers, ordered to encounter an unexplored country,* inhabited by a warlike people, inimical to the Company, occupying fastesses and defiles, and intersected by large navigable rivers, which would continually expose the army to be cut off by the sword, reduced by famine, or perish in the hospitals.

A letter from the Court of Directors, dated the 4th July, 1777, to the Presidency of Bombay, having arrived in Calcutta on the 12th March, 1778, "*parti-* "*cularly and positively confirming the treaty made by Co-* "*lonel Upton with the Marrattas, and ordering a strict* "*adherence to it; recommending special vigilance, whilst* "*Ragoba was at Bombay, that he formed no plans, against* "*what is called the ministerial party at Poonah; and po-* "*sitively commanding, that no intervention or scheme in* "*his favour, shall be entered into, without the previous* "*consent of the Supreme Council, or Court of Directors.* At the same time, saying, "*that common humanity war-* "*ranted the protection of Ragoba's person from violence.*" No council being then sitting, or to sit in the rotation of business until the Monday following, and the detachment

---

* Comprehending a space of 1500 miles.

tachment under Colonel Leslie being under orders to march, Mr. Francis and Mr. Wheler addressed the Governor General by letter on the same day, urging the Board to countermand the march, but without effect.

On the 18th March, a letter to the Presidency of Bombay, drawn up by Mr. Hastings, was laid before the Board, consisting of orders and instructions for the guidance of that Presidency. This letter is enveloped with so much art and subtilty, that though the writer's judgment must be condemned upon the face of every fact, yet a person unacquainted with the history, his views, and abilities in that way, would be apt to acquit him of having had intentions directly foreign to the language expressed. It is like the horizontal plan or base of a rugged or hilly country, laid down by outlines upon a fair sheet of paper, which deceives the eye into a belief, that the country is as flat and level as it appears represented on the paper.—It sets out with an abstract of the Company's last recited letter, which in the 65th paragraph strongly desires the observance of the treaty; and in the same breath, he charges the Marrattas with an absolute violation of every article in the treaty, with forming French connections; and insinuates a firm hope, that the spirit of the measures conveyed in the present letter of instruction, shall have been anticipated before it reaches, by a great event against the Marratta administration in favour of Roganaut-row. But, he says, as the reverse is yet probable, they (the Supreme Council) shall furnish such instructions and authority for their guidance, as are necessary on a supposition that no revolution hath taken place at Poonah, consisting of seven articles, to the following effect, *viz.*

The

The 1st requires a peremptory demand of a country of three complete lacks of rupees annual revenue, near Baroach; and in case of non-conformity, *to declare it a violation of treaty.*

The 2d requires a peremptory demand of the immediate payment of twelve lacks of rupees; and in case of non-compliance, *to declare it a violation of treaty.*

The 3d orders them to keep possession of the several villages, and pergunnahs ceded to the Company by Futta-Sing-Guicawar, *as the Marrattas have neglected to produce proofs of Futta-Sing's incapacity to make such cession.*

The 4th directs them, to remonstrate against the countenance afforded to Mr. St. Lubin; the engagements entered into with him; the grant of the port of Choul; and to demand a clear and satisfactory explanation of their intentions in regard to France.—And to declare, that the English Company shall take such measures as prudence shall dictate for the future safety of their interests and possessions. The Governor condescended to acknowledge on this subject,—" *That he* " *regarded the Marrattas as the only native, and the French* " *as the only foreign power in India, capable of affecting the* " *influence which the British nation had acquired in it.** *The* " *former having been rendered incapable by internal distrac-* " *tion,† and the inequality of their numbers to European dis-* " *cipline; and the latter, by the want of territorial pro-* " *perty, or any to supply it.—That therefore an alliance be-* " *tween them would at once relieve all their mutual wants,* " *and afford them all the requisites to dispute with us on equal* " *terms*

---

* Yet he laboured to *unite* these two powers, which were *severally* capable of affecting the British influence.

† Which distractions, his measures have healed, and effectually composed.

" terms, the dominion of India, which at present we possess
" without a rival, and may be attended with calamities more
" dreadful by the superior magnitude of the contest, than that
" which we formerly experienced in the Carnatic."*

The 5th directs them to demand a safe passage for, and assistance to Colonel Leslie's detachment, through the Marratta dominions; and to assure them, that no act of hostility shall be committed by the army on their march; and to repeat the strongest assurances of a pacific disposition and adherence to the treaty in every point.

The 6th requires the observance of the Company's orders in their last recited letter, whether the administration of Saccaram Baboo, and Nana-furnese continues, or a revolution should have taken place. But if either administration shall *directly* or *indirectly*, infringe the treaty, in such case, the Supreme Council, in virtue of their authority, *doth authorise the Bombay Council to form a new alliance with Roganaut-row, and engage with him in any expedient scheme for retrieving his affairs. And the like authority is extended*, at all events, *if they are invited to accomplish the propositions transmitted to them on the 2d of February last.*

The 7th is a general recommendation, having a clear tendency to delude and circumvent the people of Bombay, and to make them ostensible for any unfortunate event that may arise; but it artfully recommends "*such
" a policy, as circumstances will warrant, independent of any
" particular interest of Roganaut-row, whom they must re-
" gard in the great political object of our government, as sim-
" ply*

---

* What fatal confessions were these, and how inconsistent were his uniform measures, to these dreaded consequences, and to sound policy!

"ply meriting our confideration, and not neceffarily connect-
"ed or blended with them."

Inftructions and orders, thus carrying in every ex-
preffion, violence and hoftility, tantamount to a declaration of war, produced deliberate protefts from Mr.
Francis and Mr. Wheler, with fuch ftrong and folid
reafons, as obviate the propriety of any other comment.

Mr. *Francis* concurred in two general principles *profeffed* in the intended letter. Firft, to make the Directors laft letter, the ground work. And, fecondly,
to make the eftablifhment of a lafting peace, the fole
general object. On the preamble of the Governor's
letter, Mr. Francis obferved, " *that we continued in the
" peaceable poffeffion of Salfette, and of the Marratta fhare
" of the city and pergunnah of Baroach as ftipulated by
" treaty.*"

I. As to the firft article inftructive, he alledged, that
its execution appeared to have been retarded, only by
a difpute about the literal meaning of a word,* differ-
ently conftrued by each party; and that the admiffion
by the Supreme Board, on the 18th Auguft laft, of
grofs inftead of *neat* revenue, decided the difpute in favour of the Marrattas. But that having feveral other
places in poffeffion, and enjoying their revenues, as
pledges, until the grants of the whole country required
were made out, our fecurity was not affected by any
delay, occafioned chiefly by that difpute.

II. That by the acceptance and poffeffion of Jam-
boofeer in mortgage, to be held until the revenues collected from thence, fhall have liquidated the debt of
twelve

* Kaumil Jumma,

twelve lacks, which the Marrattas had confented to pay us towards the charge of the late war, demanded in the fecond inftruction, it muft be conftrued as a mutual performance of the treaty.

III. That the third inftruction, deciding arbitrarily, and *ex parte*, the right of Futta Sing to make the ceffion therein fpecified, which appeared to him (Mr. Francis) very difputable; if decided after this imperious manner in our own favour, would make the eftablifhment of a *lafting peace* impoffible.

IV. That the fourth inftruction, fuppofed the port of Choul to have been ceded to the French, an affertion which had already been acknowledged, upon enquiry, to want proof; and that the menaces uttered, if anfwers confonant to the defires of the Prefidency of Bombay, or of Mr. Haftings and Mr. Barwell, were not returned, amounted to a declaration of war: Mr. Francis obferved, "*That the Marrattas having thus conformed to the conditions of the treaty, it feemed juft and reafonable, that fome fatisfaction fhould be given them on our fide; particularly, that Roganaut-row fhould be removed from Bombay, with a proper provifion for his eftablifhment in a private ftation; that if any negociations were formed with the French, we may trace them to their fource, in the protection given to Roganaut-row, his refidence at Bombay, and the continued intrigues between him and that Prefidency; that the true way to defeat the views of France, was to give the Marrattas a folid proof of our good faith; that while Roganaut-row, a pretender to their government, was fupported by us, we give them too much caufe for looking to France for affiftance; and that the prefent meafures will leave them without a choice.*"

V. As

V. As to the fifth inftruction, after ftating the contradiction, and motives, which on different occafions have been affigned for fending an army to Bombay, he afked, "*If permiſſion for a ſafe paſſage and aſſiſtance is refuſed, ſhall the detachment, nevertheleſs, be ordered to march through the Marratta territory, againſt their declared inclinations? And if that is meant, whether that act alone does not conſtitute a declaration of war, which cannot be qualified by any aſſurances of our pacific intentions? That ſuch language, united with ſuch meaſures, is an inſult to common ſenſe, and much too plain to deceive, either the Marrattas or the Court of Directors.*"

VI. On the fixth inftruction, leaving an option in the Bombay Prefidency, whether to declare the treaty infringed, by the Marrattas, or by themfelves, and in confequence of fuch decifion, impowering them to enter into new engagements with Roganaut-row, for retrieving his affairs with effect, he faid, "*That, in the preſent temper and diſpoſition of that Preſidency, there cannot be a doubt of the uſe they will make of this extraordinary power, or that they will not be forward to avail themſelves of it, before it can be re-called.*"

VII. On the feventh inftruction, which leaves the Prefidency of Bombay in poffeffion of deciding as they fhall pleafe, and recommends the intereft of Roganaut-row to be regarded only as unconnected with the grand political fyftem,* he faid, "*It is a manifeſt contradiction to the foregoing, and to former inſtructions; That not to purſue ſome one determinate ſyſtem may be hazardous and diſgraceful: That he conceived the Supreme Board not warranted to convey ſuch unlimited powers to the Preſidency of Bombay: That that Preſidency ſhould continue*

D "*ſubor-*

---

* Mr. Haftings never communicated this "grand political fyftem" to the Prefidency of Bombay.

"subordinate, and be successively directed by the Supreme
" Council; and that the peace of India, perhaps the fate of
" the British empire in this part of the world, is involved
" in the questions, which are thus left to their future deci-
" sions." He asked, " Are we justified in relinquishing
" our jurisdiction, even for a moment, over such ques-
" tions?" And he concluded thus: " Upon the whole,
" it appears to me, that the real tendency of this letter, not-
" withstanding any qualifying expressions interspersed through
" it, is to provoke a war with the Marrattas; that it
" seeks for causes of offence, where none exist; that the lan-
" guage it holds to the Marrattas is peremptory and hostile,
" and never used but when a rupture is pre-determined;
" that the causes of complaint on which it urges a quarrel,
" are trifling and exaggerated; that the facts it refers to,
" are either clearly disproved, or taken for granted, with-
" out evidence; and that the terms of the instructions are
" in some places ambiguous, and in others contradictory.—
" Whether they are or are not consistent with the pacific re-
" solutions, so clearly and positively expressed by the Court
" of Directors, in their letter of the 4th July, must be left
" to their judgment."

Mr. *Wheler* having repeated his dissent and protesta-
tion against any interference between the contending
powers of the Marratta government, and the armament
then under orders for Bombay, as well as the purpose
to which it was to be employed, declared, " That he
" should not think it necessary in future to enter into discus-
" sions on these matters, as the Governor General and Mr.
" Barwell had taken the whole responsibility on themselves;
" must be answerable for the consequences of the measures al-
" ready resolved on, and such as may, of necessity, follow."*
He agreed with the Governor, that the 65th paragraph
of

---

* In justice, and in good policy, should not the private estates of persons taking responsibility upon themselves, in such strong instances, which, in the letter of law, may amount to an assumption of debt, be held accountable, in terms thereof, for the consequences?

of the Company's letter to Bombay shou'd be the ground of the instructions to that Presidency, but he dissented from every other part of them, on the same principles as those urged by Mr. Francis.

Mr. *Barwell* having joined in the Governor's measures, the letter was prepared, and agreed to, for signature and dispatch.

Colonel Goddard's regiment of cavalry were ordered, on the 30th March, to join Colonel Leslie's detachment, and to proceed to Bombay.

Advices from Bombay, received the 6th April, represented every thing in a state of perfect tranquility; that no motion had been made in favour of Roganautrow, nor measure arisen from the pretended overtures of his partizans in Poonah, mentioned in their letter of 12th December. Yet Colonel Leslie's detachment was ordered to march; instructions were passed; from all of which Mr. Francis and Mr. Wheler dissented. Several minutes by Mr. Hastings, in reply to Mr. Francis, with rejoinders and sur-rejoinders, explanatory of former minutes, and quibbling upon words, were committed to record, in the course of this month, but so immaterial as not to merit quotation.

The object of this narrative being restrained to such facts and circumstances, as shall remove false impressions from misrepresentations, and to shew the unwearied, unremitted, and faithful resistance made by Mr. Francis and Mr. Wheler, through each and every stage of the ruinous business. So alarming were these gentlemens apprehensions, and such their prescience of the declining state of the Company's finances, as well as those of their *dependent* allies in India, the probable wants of the nation in Europe, and the demand which the nation must make, in some shape or other, on the Company,

Company, for a renewal of their charter, to answer the calls of a general war, so much threatened in Europe, that the records exhibit indefatigable labour and assiduity in both, and marks of nervous, clear, and irresistible abilities in Mr. Francis, to oppose expences, and to introduce principles of œconomy, on every occasion; and that it was with these views, and those of justice, together with a fixed intention to good-faith, and the preservation of national fame, that he uniformly and steadily pressed, without intermission, against the Marratta war, and every other avoidable hostility in India; as most consistent with the instructions of the Company, with good policy, and with honour. Lest it should be alledged, that this detachment was not attended with an extraordinary military charge of magnitude, it is proper to assert, as a truth, that an equal number of troops were immediately recruited, by additional battalions, and an augmentation of each existing battalion, at an immense expence in advance, cloathing, arms, and discipline; and that an extra staff, extra stores, extra train of artillery, and other unforeseen extra expences, incident to such an occasion, besides the charges and actual losses upon the exchange of remittances, together also with the distressing irretrievable inconveniency of transporting the current coins wanted in circulation at home, into parts from whence it cannot return. Even the distresses of the Nabob of Oude were heightened; and the Rajah Cheyt Sing, the identical tributary of the Company, had a new contribution levied upon him, under this pretext, in addition to his established tribute. Demands equally unjust and impolitic, as they were compulsatory, at a time, when prudence should have dictated the propriety, perhaps the necessity, of conciliating the minds, attaching the affections, and securing the loyalty and fidelity of the principal natives, instead of creating disaffections and resentments, by claims which were not founded on precontracts, or conditional treaties, but upon the capricious

cious movements of imperious and oppreſſive minds, having, in remote as well as immediate contemplation, ends very oppoſite to thoſe which were profeſſed.

May 11, 1778. Advices from Bombay of the 5th April, having communicated the accounts of a revolution at Poonah, in favour of Roganaut-row,* Mr. Francis, upon a principle that any aſſiſtance from Bengal would not now be wanted on the Malabar coaſt, either againſt the Marrattas, or to oppoſe France, as the ſuppoſed connection between Nana-furneſe and Monſieur St. Lubin could no longer exiſt with effect, reſumed the ſubject of ſuſpending the march of Colonel Leſlie's detachment, as no longer neceſſary. But the Governor perſiſted as before, and over-ruled the motion.

May 16. The detachment having marched, and the rainy ſeaſon approaching, Mr. Francis urged the recall of the detachment. Mr. Haſtings, with conſtant perſeverance, againſt his own knowledge and certain conviction, maintained, " *That no ſeaſon could be more happily choſen than the beginning of May; that the violent heats would ſoon be over; and that the ſucceeding rains would be a relief to the troops, and facilitate the march.*"—To thoſe who have experienced the rains of India, the idea will appear new and extraordinary. Colonel Leſlie's letters, *particularly his private ones to the Governor*, prove that nothing could have been ſo ill founded. He uniformly attributes the delay of his march to the torrents of rain which had overflowed the country, deſtroying the roads, and making even the ſmall rivers and guts impaſſable. Light troops, without incumbrance, may perhaps move in any ſeaſon, but it is not ſo eaſy to convey a train of artillery, with ſtores, ammunition, camp-equipage, and
provisions,

---

* This was falſe.

provisions, for a body of people not less than 38,000 in number, in a tempestuous season, and through an enemy's country, intersected with numberless streams, generally overflowed. The effect of the heat was fatally experienced on the first day's march from Calpee; by the ignorance of the conductors, or the obstinacy of the commander, they moved out of the right course, and for want of water, and through fatigue, between 300 and 400 persons, belonging to the army, or to its followers, died raving mad. Captain Crawford, one of the best and bravest characters in India, died in that state, of two hours illness. Colonel Parker, Major Fullarton, Captain Ash, Captain Showers, and about ten subalterns, happily recovered from dangerous illnesses, occasioned by the march. And when Colonel Goddard, after the death of Colonel Leslie, took charge of the army, although very little progress had been made in the route, he found above a thousand Sepoys in the hospital.

June 8. By letters from Colonel Leslie, it is discovered, that the Marratta states adjoining to the Jumna, had opposed the passing of the army, and continued a resistance through the Bundlecund country; that Moodajee Boosla, Rajah of Berar, had expressed an unwillingness to admit the detachment near his capital, the evident effect of distrust; that he disclaimed all political interests and objects for himself; that he refused to join his troops with the Company's; and that he recommended, in the strongest terms, an accommodation with the Marrattas, offering himself as a mediator. Mr. Francis renewed his motion for the recall of the detachment, on account of the opposition and obstruction it had already received, and the further difficulties it would meet with. — The Governor's reply merits particular attention; he described the route of the army with so minute a direction, and with so positive a security,

curity, through Bundlecund and Bapaul; he afferted fo confidently, the invitation and prefling folicitations of Moodajee Boofla to fend the army through his country; and declared fo pointedly the political objects and interefts of that prince, that one would forbear even to doubt the moral poffibility of the facts alledged. He infinuated that the Marratta tribes were not under fubjection to the Paifhwa; in order to imprefs an idea of their unimportance, as a ftate capable of annoying the march of the detachment.—What muft Mr. Haftings's warmeft adherents and advocates now think of his political judgement and affeverations, againft proofs fo incontrovertibly pofitive, if they pretend to vindicate his intentions?

Mr. Francis rejoined, in an able and fpirited minute, to all Mr. Haftings's equivocations, fophiftry, and ill-founded affertions. — He obferved, That whether the Marrattas, as diftinct tribes, are under immediate fubjection to the Paifhwa or not, was very immaterial, when a general alliance, and a common enemy, operated on their interefts and mutual fecurity.

Mr. Haftings fur-rejoined, in terms that muft have ftruck the Directors with aftonifhment, if they attended to the expreffions, and their inequivocal tendency, by which he declared " *his unalterable determination to pro-*
" *fecute the meafure to the utmoft of his power to the con-*
" *clufion.*" — He faid, " *That the difgrace of thofe who*
" *planned the expedition, the irreparable lofs of the credit of*
" *this government, and a perpetual diftruft of all its future*
" *acts, exclufive of the forfeiture of the advantages for*
" *which it was originally concerted, would be the infallible*
" *confequence of ftopping the expedition.*" Do not thefe words mark, in ftrong terms, and diftinguifhed characters, the obftinate and imperious difpofition of the man, which is not to be with-held from its purpofes,
by

by self-evident consequences, or immediate danger? But " *a thirst for plunder, and an avidity for power, have ever been motives of hostility and injustice, to avaricious men,*" is the sentiment of a very sensible, intelligent person,* one of Hastings's principal agents, in a late publication, "*Of the History and Management of the East-India Company*," which is peculiarly applicable to the author's own friend.

By letters received the 11th June, from Bombay, dated the 2d May, they advise, that they had countermanded the advance of Colonel Leslie's detachment, until further orders. — That this step was founded on the opinion they had formed of the present state of affairs, and their desire to rescue the Company from the heavy expence, and their troops from the dangers and difficulties of a march from Bengal to Bombay.

By letters of the 9th May, received the 21st June, they advise of having reversed the last-mentioned resolution, within two days after the measure was adopted; and that they had ordered Colonel Leslie to proceed. But they assigned no reason for the alteration.

June 22. Considering this extraordinary fluctuation and unsteadiness in the Council of Bombay, and that no motives whatsoever were assigned for it, Mr. Francis represented to the Board, the hazard and discredit of leaving a detachment at the discretion of such Council; and, on that ground, urged again, but in vain, the necessity of recalling it.

June 29. Another letter from Bombay advised the receipt of Instructions from the Supreme Council, and that, in consequence thereof, they had directed Mr. Mostyn

* Mr. John Macpherson.

Moftyn to demand, from the Regency of Poonah, the several matters ordered by the Governor-general and Council. — That, conceiving the paſſage of Colonel Leſlie's detachment to be attended with almoſt inſuperable dangers and difficulties, they recommended, that in future, any reinforcement to them might proceed directly from Madras, as the beſt and eaſieſt mode. — Thus, it is evident to demonſtration, that the ſafety of the detachment was more the effect of chance than conduct.

July 6. The detachment having croſſed the Jumna, and proceeded into the heart of a hoſtile country, from whence its recall might be conſtrued into a diſgraceful defeat and retreat, the Governor thought it no longer neceſſary to diſguiſe his real purpoſes; on the 6th of July, he dropt the maſk, by the firſt direct move towards the object which he ſince appears to have had originally at heart, of an alliance with the Rajah of Berar, and which will appear to have been, (notwithſtanding the reaſons oſtenſibly held out) the real object of the expedition. The myſtery once unfolded, all further concealments were either uſeleſs or impracticable.—The great difficulty with Mr. Haſtings appears to have been, to find pretences for ſo extraordinary and queſtionable a ſtep, as that of ſending the Company's troops out of the provinces, over land to the oppoſite extremity of India, againſt the very letter of repeated and poſitive orders, and to account for the enormous expences that muſt attend it. To remove thoſe difficulties, no aſſertions were ſpared, no artifice omitted, and no ſophiſtry unemployed. That point once carried, and the army out of the probable reach of being recalled,—new facts are aſſerted, new principles eſtabliſhed, and new objects propoſed.— The ſame army, which originally was to have reinſtated Roganaut-row, and to ſupport that intereſt alone, is now deſtined

destined to place Moodajee Boosla at the head of the Marratta empire, as well in opposition to Roganautrow as to his adversaries; and the Company to join with that prince in invading the dominions of their own ally, the Nizam of the Deccan. And yet Mr. Hastings, in the month of December following, declared, that this Moodajee Boosla, who was then dangerously ill, and expected to die, and who was to have been exalted to the Marratta Imperial throne, was not the real Rajah of Berar, nor the pretender to the Ramrajah-ship, but the Naib, or Deputy Rajah of Berar, during the minority of the real prince. In consequence of this change in the destination of the expedition, Colonel Leslie was ordered to take his route through Berar, instead of pursuing the direct easy road through Malva; and, for the first time, Madajee Scindia, the chief of that district, was declared by Mr. Hastings, to have had no friendly intercourse or connection with the Company; and that he was always represented as a partizan with Nana-furnese, against them, and in favour of the French.

July 7. Advice arrived from Mr. Baldwin, the Company's agent at Cairo, on the 7th July, which, however, proved premature, that war had been declared between France and Britain.—Mr. Francis recurred to his original motion, and urged the necessity, in consequence of that event, of recalling the detachment for the defence and protection of the Company's principal object. The Governor and Mr. Barwell persisted as before, and ordered it to halt in Berar; while the Presidency of Bombay were, by order of these very persons who compose the majority, declaring war, and committing hostilities, on the faith of receiving assistance from this very detachment, which, for that sole purpose, *ostensibly*, was put under their absolute authority.

July

July 9. At a time when, in confequence of the advices from Cairo, it was expected that the defence of the Company's poffeffions would occupy the deliberations of the Supreme Council, to fecure their dominion and trade againſt French invaſions, Mr. Haſtings produced a laboured hiſtory of the Ram-rajah, the conſtitution of the Marratta empire, and ſome remote pretenſions of Moodajee Boofla, by confanguinity, to the Marratta ſovereignty. And concluded with a propoſal to enter into a treaty with Moodajee Boofla, who (he alledged) was at *perpetual* and *inveterate warfare* with the Regency of Poonah, and with the Soubah of the Deccan, with whom the Company were yet in terms of friendſhip by alliance and ſolemn treaties. And that a Company's ſervant ſhould be immediately difpatched to him, with plenipotentiary powers to that purpoſe.

A ſyſtem of policy ſo contrary to common ſenſe, common juſtice, and common faith, is difficult to be juſtified. If the Marrattas with a French alliance, were acknowledged by Mr. Haſtings, " *to be capable of refuſing acquieſcence to,*" and " *obſtructing upon an equality of power, the Britiſh views in Hindoſtan,*" what muſt the ſame power, in conjunction with the Soubah, who is the richeſt prince in India, and the probable junction of the Soubah's moſt particular friend and infeparable ally Hyder-Alli-Cawn, produce to the Company's difadvantage, toward the total fubverſion of the Britiſh empire in Aſia? Muſt not ſuch meaſures render the Marrattas, not only irreconcileable and inveterate, but deſperate? Would not the union of theſe three powerful ſtates, eaſily overrun the Carnatic, and reſtore to the Soubah the five northern Circars, which the Company now enjoy? And after the reduction of all the Company's forts and garriſons on each ſide of the peninſula, would not that united power confine the remaining influence of the Company

Company to the Bengal provinces, and perhaps render *them* insecure? Such an event, considering the shackles which the Company have impolitically held upon their allies in the interior countries, and the pinioned princes of the Carnatic, would, without a deviation from good faith and honour, rejoice their hearts, in the prospect which a native superiority would offer to their emancipation and enfranchisement.

July 10. Mr. Francis and Mr. Wheler, on the 10th July, argued against the proposals of Mr. Hastings on the preceding day, and urged the necessity of putting Bengal in a state of defence, recalling the detachment, and sending a reinforcement from Madras to Bombay; *to act solely on a defensive plan.*

July 11. The next day, the subject was revived and canvassed, with a motion for recalling the detachment. Mr. Wheler desired time to consider the nature and extent of the intended treaty, before he positively determined; in which he was joined by Mr. Francis. The majority resolved on a treaty, and that Mr. Elliot be appointed to negociate it. The plan was not produced.

July 18. Mr. Hastings having prepared powers and instructions for Mr. Elliot's embassy to Berar, produced them at the Board the 18th July, and were voted by himself and Mr. Barwell against a strenuous opposition by Mr. Francis and Mr. Wheler. * It appeared upon these documents, that the treaty was to extend generally, to offence and defence; that Roganaut-row was to be set aside; that Moodajee Boosla was to be placed at the head of the Marratta empire, and to be supported in his pretensions against the Company's ally, the Soubah

---

* Mr. Wheler's minute is strong, pathetic, and sensible, against the treaty and the expedition.

bah of the Deccan. This plan of new, hostile, and extensive operations, which instantly tended to involve all India, was proposed and urged by Mr. Hastings, at the beginning of a French war, and at a time that all India beheld the Company's growing power and usurpations with fearful, jealous eyes, without any availing and direct measure taken or proposed, for the effectual security of Bengal, or any other of the Company's possessions † During all this time, the detachment halted at Chatterpore, a few days march from the Jumna. It appeared from Col. Leslie's letters, that Mr. Hastings must have been perfectly acquainted with all the transactions of the army; particularly in his letter of 30th June, where he says, " *That he will critically observe the Governor's private instructions, in communicating with him, one post before he does with the Board; in order that he may have time to observe upon it, before it reaches the Board, &c.*" Yet at the Board, the Governor constantly defended him, and recommended to the Board to approve Colonel Leslie's violent and hostile attack upon the town and fortress of Mow, under the protection of the Marrattas, although the Governor could not but be acquainted with the true motives of that barbarous depredatory measure.

August 17. A letter from Bombay, dated 25th July, was received in Calcutta the 17th Aug. saying, " *That they had declared the treaty of Poonah violated, and no longer binding on the Company; that they had determined to accept the offers of Moraba and other Chiefs, who had declared in favour of Roganautrow;*

---

† To save appearances at home, and to gloss over his own measures, Mr. Hastings proposed several unavailing and ineffectual modes preparatory to defence; while, at the same time, he connived at dismantling the grand arsenal of the actual arms. A narrative of transactions in the ordnance department will appear in support of this allegation.

"row; and accordingly had determined to accompany
"him with an army to Poonah, the beginning of Sep-
"tember." Notwithstanding Mr. Hastings's projected
treaty with Moodajee Boosla, he warmly approved the
plan for reinstating Roganaut-row; yet he represented
Roganaut-row's cause as desperate, and the measures of
the Presidency of Bombay, " *as equivalent to a reso-*
" *lution to do nothing.*" The meaning of which is,
that he supported measures which he knew would not
take effect. But, probably, he trusted that they might
save his projected detachment, at the hazard of the
Bombay army, Bombay itself, and all the Company's
factories on that side of India. By letters from Colonel
Leslie it appeared, that the gentlemen of Bombay had
directed him to proceed in a direct course to Poonah,
instead of the route through Guzzerat to Baroach, or
Surat, as had been pre-determined.

In council, on the 31st August, some reflections having been made by Mr. Francis on Colonel Leslie's extraordinary delay at Chatterpore, the Board agreed with
him, that the causes deserved to be enquired into.

And on the 2d September, in the course of a warm
debate on the stay of the detachment at Chatterpore,
Mr. Hastings uniformly defended and supported Colonel Leslie, and with much apparent confidence in his
conduct, referred to the event to justify it. It afterwards appeared from the letters of Colonel Leslie, that
all these defences were fallacious and deceitful. In a
letter dated at Chatterpore, the 30th July, Colonel
Leslie tells Mr. Hastings, bluntly, " *That he had the*
" *Governor's own private and public approbation of all the*
" *measures, which he had since condemned and execrated*
" *bitterly.*" He added, " *that he hopes for the Governor's*
" *own reputation, that he believes the assertions of ignorance,*
" *presumption, and rapacity, imputed to him (the Colonel)*
" *in*

' in Captain Palmer's letter, to be true, for the following
' lines in the same letter from Capt. Palmer to Capt. Cocke-
' rell, say, That *my disgrace is determined on, either by the
' recall of the detachment, or by my supercession in the com-
' mand; and that the efforts of friendship alone, not a
' possibility of my being innocent of these charges, protracts
' the measure, and suspends your resolution.*" This quotation from Captain Palmer's letter must have been very early in July, or the latter end of June. It manifestly proves, that the most sacred trusts were sacrificed to private views, and private friendships, as the declarations by the Governor's most confidential secretary, must have had his authority.

From the 22d September to the 5th October, no material advices from Colonel Leslie had transpired. He had altered the position of his camp, but without any apparent intention to pursue the march. The hostility committed by him in the province of Bundlecund (*the Country of Diamonds*) being as reprehensible as the delay, and other circumstances, Mr. Francis urged again, that his conduct should be enquired into; but at the particular request of Mr. Hastings, *to defer it*, that influence predominated. Having received accounts of the death of Mr. Elliot, in his way to negociate the treaty with the Rajah of Berar, Mr. Hastings moved in council, that the commission be continued, and another person appointed to carry it into execution.

It is a justice due to superior merit, to digress in this place, in order to lament the too early fate of one of the most promising characters, and elevated genius, which dignify humanity; and to sympathize with his relations and acquaintances; for all who knew him were his friends, as well as strangers, to whom report only yielded an opportunity of admiring his virtues and capacity,

pacity, for the death of Alexander Elliot, Esq.* He fell a martyr to patriotism, and fidelity to his employers.— Afflicted with a disorder peculiar to the East, which originates in bilious obstructions, and in the cure requires too copious an application of mercury; his duty (as he thought) prevailed over reason, in undertaking a long and harrassing journey, in the deluged season, without the possibility of accommodations suited to his state. After leaving the Company's territories, he discovered that Governor Chevalier, who had secretly escaped from Chandernagore, was pursuing the same route, before him. Knowing the ambitious designs of that man, and the accurate knowledge he had acquired in the politics of India, these suggestions instigated Mr. Elliot to endeavour, at all events, to seize his person, dreading that his liberty and arrival in France might be attended with the worst consequences to the Company's affairs, and the views of Britain, in India. He moved on by forced and fatiguing journeys, still tracing and approaching Mr. Chevalier.— Unfortunately, when he had the chace in view, one of the large rivers of Catac, obstructed his progress, by a sudden overflow of its waters. Zeal and resolution actuated him, regardless of the state of his body, and the medicines which he had used, and the exertion of strength and activity which the stemming of a rapid stream required, he undertook and succeeded, in swimming over the river, with a few of his attendants and sepoys.— He found Mr. Chevalier at the metropolis of Catac; and although escorted only by a company of sepoys, he claimed the person of Governor Chevalier from the Rajah, with such sensible and manly arguments in support thereof, that the Rajah yielded to Mr. Elliot's eloquence, as superior to that of Mr. Chevalier, and surrendered him up. As Mr. Elliot had but a
small

* Son to the late Sir Gilbert Elliot.

small escort, and the longest and most dangerous part of his journey yet to encounter, he could not, without sacrificing the object of his commission, return a guard to conduct Mr. Chevalier and his companion Mr. Moneron to Calcutta; therefore he engaged their paroles in writing, to surrender themselves as prisoners of war within a limitted time, to the Governor-general. — Mr. Chevalier and Mr. Moneron performed their engagements; Mr. Elliot pursued his route for Berar, and died a few days thereafter. Thus, by an exertion worthy of Mr. Elliot, did he lose his own life, the Company a most able and faithful servant, and his country a loyal subject. And Mr. Hastings, with opposite sentiments, accommodated his friend Mr. Chevalier, with a safe and speedy passage to Versailles. A mode of conveyance which Mr. Chevalier could not have atchieved in thrice the time, if at all, had he been suffered to wander through the interior of India in disguise.

On the 7th October, Mr. Hastings withdrew his motion for continuing the commission, and sending another person to execute it; but he persisted, notwithstanding, in forming the alliance with Moodajee Boosla. Although he had discovered, and, in consequence thereof, declared, "*That it was always more advantageous to wait for solicitations, than to make advances.*"

The new instructions *now* proposed for the march of the detachment, will be found to deserve particular attention.* The tendency of them was, that the detachment should be left under the orders of the Presidency of Bombay, for the express purposes of supporting any plan or design for the restoration of Roganaut-row, and to provide for the immediate safety

---

* Vide the minute upon record.

of Bombay, against a French invasion. Upon this occasion, Mr. Hastings, for the first time, avowed a distrust of Colonel Leslie, with an indirect profession of an intention to remove him.

October 12. However important the subject, considering the charge and power with which Colonel Leslie was intrusted, no resolution was taken to remove him from the command, until the 12th October.—Mr. Hastings, upon that occasion, informed the Board, " *That it had been the will of God to blast his designs by* " *means which no human prudence could have foreseen, and* " *against which he had therefore provided no resource.*" Yet he affirmed, " *That the effects of the detachment will* " *still answer his most sanguine hopes, and that the measure* " *itself is as adviseable now, and more so, than when it* " *was first adopted.*" Mr. Francis, with his wonted zeal, by a most able minute, urged against meddling, directly or indirectly, in the differences and pretensions of the Marratta chiefs and ministers amongst themselves. * " He briefly recapitulated his continued and invariable opposition to a cause, and measures, so inconsistent with sound policy, and the real interests and security of the Company's possessions and trade, through every

---

* The Company's positive injunctions in the general letter to Madras, dated 27th June, 1770, against offensive and officious alliances, are peculiarly adapted to the sentiments expressed by Mr. Francis, viz. " *We have only here to enjoin you, to avoid, as much* " *as in you lies, becoming parties in any dispute between the powers* " *in India; and to pay the most strict obedience to our orders, for* " *confining our views to our present possessions; the peace and se-* " *curity of which are the utmost scope of our wishes; as they will* " *necessarily tend to advance the commercial and vital interests of the* " *Company*"

Mr. Hastings was second in Council at Madras, upon the 18th April, 1771, when this letter was quoted in clear and satisfactory justification of the sentiments and conduct of that Board, and, for that purpose, entered upon their proceedings.

every succeffive stage thereof. He stated the disappointment and failure in the pretended support of Roganaut-row and his partizans, their dispersion, and the imprisonment of his principal adherents in Poonah.—That, by advice from Colonel Leslie, the detachment, in four months, had only marched 120 miles, at the expence of 12 lacks of rupees, or 3 lacks per month; that they were opposed by a numerous body of Marrattas and natives; and that they had yet above a thousand miles to march over." Mr. Francis then desired information on several interesting points—How money was to be supplied?—how provisions were to be conveyed?—what probability there was, that the Rajah of Berar would receive and entertain them as friends and *allies*, or give them a passage through his country? or even, admitting these facts to be resolved favourably, "Whether Mr. Hastings believes confidently, that if the army shall meet with no interruption in its march, it will get to Bombay, in time to afford relief to that place, if it shall be attacked, or that an attack had been preconcerted by the allied forces of the French and the Marrattas?" It is a truth well known, that it is with violence to themselves, and difficulty to their officers, that seapoys will embark upon the sea, if at all. If the army had marched, as was originally intended, to Baroach or Surat, which are in the Guzzerat country, their distance from Bombay would not only be very great, but more difficult, by reason of almost inaccessible defiles and passes between hills; and the entire space inhabited by a numerous martial people, in that degree that they could not yield more speedy succours to Bombay, than if they were cantoned in the Bengal provinces.

October 19. Chatterpore, which is the capital of Bundlecund, is situate near the western confine of that province. Its distance from Calcutta may be computed at twenty days ordinary journey for a native courier.

Here the detachment had long lain. Col. Leslie's last letter was laid before the Board upon the 19th October, wherein he stated the causes which retarded his march, and accounts for his not having being heretofore more explicit in his communication to the Board, saying, "*That he had furnished Mr. Hastings, at his own special desire, a particular journal of occurrences, and therefore had trusted to him for such explanations as the Board might desire to know.*" The Colonel expressed no apprehension of Mr. Hastings's resentment, or of any effects it could produce; but, on the contrary, sets him at open defiance in plain terms, and refused to hold private correspondence with him any longer.

October 22. The Governor having received intimation of the death of Colonel Leslie at Chatterpore, on the 3d October, laid that information, and the Colonel's private letters, before the Board, on the 22d; although the event had been known in the native circle of Calcutta, and therefore to the Governor, most probably, several days before; and it is a general conjecture, that the impossibility of his recovery was effectually established as an inevitable consequence, in the Governor's mind, at the time he consented to his dismission from the command of the army, on the 12th October.

November 2. Colonel Goddard, as second, having succeeded to the chief command of the detachment, upon the death of Colonel Leslie, he advised that he found the military treasure-chest empty; that he was obliged to draw bills for the subsistence of his troops; that there were upwards of 1000 sepoys in the hospital; and that, under these inconveniences, he had, notwithstanding, proceeded on his march to Sagur.

On the 12th November, the Governor proposed an arrangement for supplying the detachment with money by remittances to Nagpore, the capital of Berar.—If it was not intended that the army shall halt in that country, the measure was absurd, because if the detachment was to march without interruption to Bombay, it would be arrived there before remittances from Calcutta could reach Berar. The proposition expressed an immediate want of money, and to receive it in two months from this date, at a place considerably more than a thousand miles from the place of destination. One would almost suppose, that this proposition argued deliberate purposes to waste the Company's treasures, in the same manner as the original expedition seemed calculated to consume their army.

November 6. A private letter from Colonel Goddard, of the 22d October, with others from Moodajee Boosla and his ministers, to the Governor, were laid before the Board. The Governor proposed to renew the negociation with Moodajee Boosla, on the principles of Mr. Elliot's instructions; although it was but upon the 7th of last month, that he had declared, "*It would be more advantageous to wait for solicitations than to make advances.*" And he proposed, that Colonel Goddard have charge of the negociation, with full powers to conclude.

Mr. Francis and Mr. Wheler opposed the motion, but it was carried against them.—They then objected to the private correspondence carried on between the Governor and the commanding officers of the Company's troops, thus detached out of the provinces, without any fixed destination, or principle of action.—The private mode of correspondence, so universally exacted and practised by Mr. Hastings, with the commanding officer of the detachment, ought to be as much an object

ject of confideration, as it certainly was of fufpicion. One of the objecting members obferved with great juftice, *"That it was very difficult and diftreffing to thofe members of council, who difapprove of fuch a proceeding, to exprefs their difapprobation of it, in terms that do not imply perfonal diftruft of their Prefident. There was no language (he faid) in which a total want of confidence in his perfonal honour and veracity can be conveyed, without a direct affront to him."* Mr. Francis, in his minute of this day, objected to the continuance of this correfpondence, in the moft guarded and moderate terms, and more with a view to exculpate himfelf, than from any hope of influencing Mr. Haftings's conduct.—The practice is fo evidently wrong, and fo capable of being dangerous, and alfo open to many obvious ill confequences, that it needs no illuftration.—By the private letters which Mr. Haftings produced on the 22d October, (which may have been felected, as his private letters to Colonel Leflie were not laid before the Board) it appeared that he poffeffed material information in many inftances, which ought to have had direct and immediate communication to the Governor-general and Council. The letter of 30th July in particular, eftablifhes two very interefting facts. 1ft, That, whereas Mr. Francis appears on the face of the confultations, to obferve Colonel Leflie's conduct with attention, and to cenfure it with fome degree of feverity, while Mr. Haftings conftantly fupported and defended him; it is neverthelefs true, that at leaft fo early as the end of June, Mr. Haftings muft have thought infinitely worfe of Colonel Leflie's conduct, than even Mr. Francis, who had no light to guide him, but the public letters. 2dly, That whereas Mr. Haftings, about the end of June, if not fooner, muft have conceived the very worft opinion poffible of Colonel Leflie, he took no ftep to remove him from the command till the 12th October, when, in all probability,

lity, he was thoroughly assured that there was no possibility of his recovery; if his intelligence did not amount to a certainty that he was then dead." So that, in his own principles, he must have left the conduct of this most important interprize in the hands of a man, whom he does not scruple to accuse of *ignorance, presumption, and rapacity.*

A motion was sent in circulation by the Governor, on the 23d November, to revoke the power delegated on the 19th October, to the Presidency of Bombay, of commanding the march and route of the detachment. Mr. Francis and Mr. Wheler protested against it, as not only inconsistent with all the principles hitherto avowed, and with the oftensible objects heretofore proposed to be accomplished by the expedition, but as not corresponding with, or capable of being justified, by the reasons assigned for it. Let the direction of this motion, and the reasons in support of it, be compared with the language held by Mr. Hastings, on the 12th October last, when he violently censured the Presidency of Bombay, for not pushing matters to extremity against the Marratta regency in favour of Roganaut-row, and how much pains he took to fix responsibility upon them for past and future miscarriages in the operations of the detachment: He said, " *They have done nothing. They have attempted nothing. They have neither avail-*

---

* This circumstance will admit a severe suspicion, and imply a dangerous connivance. It strongly implies a confidence of Colonel Leslie's death, before the accounts of his dismission from the command could reach Chatterpore. A violent man, impressed with resentment, and wounded by his disgrace, would be too apt to blab dangerous truths. And these suspicions are heightened by the menace and defiance which are pretty plainly couched in his late letters, particularly that of the 30th of July, where, confident of holding fast by a *secret*, on which he could rely, he shook off all restraint.

"ed themselves, nor wished to avail themselves of
"events. They have no instrument left, nor any incli-
"nation to seek for one. In short, we are abandoned
"by them, after all that we have done for their re-
"lief."—And the indignation with which he pretended on the same day to resent a suspicion expressed by
Mr. Francis, that the detachment was really never meant
to proceed to Bombay; which Mr. Hastings replied to,
in these lofty words: "*If there are men in England so
"devoid of common sense, as to suppose it possible for
"me to have formed a plan ostensibly professed for the as-
"sistance of Roganaut-row, but really meant as a cover
"for other designs, let them. Whoever they be, or in
"whatever relation they may stand to this government,
"such opinions will give me no kind of concern.*" If
these expressions were not meant as a mask upon treachery of the deepest shade, they arose from a consciousness of guilt, and premeditated abuse, which
therefore nothing but the most insulting effrontery could
brave. Indeed, they are only a specimen of his uniform conduct since the death of Sir John Clavering.

By a letter received the 30th November from Mr.
Lewis, the acting resident at Poonah, dated the 27th
October, the following information is conveyed:
"By orders from Governor Hornby, I have sent away all
"the sepoys who came with Mr. Mostyn, and am in
"hourly expectation of being recalled myself, as the Go-
"vernor writes me, that the Secret Committee have de-
"termined on acting against this government." Thus,
in virtue of the discretionary powers, and the violent and positive instructions accompanying it, which
were sent to the Presidency of Bombay on the 18th
March, *according to the prediction of Mr. Francis*, in his
remark on the 6th article of the instructions, that Presidency declared war deliberately against the Marratta
empire.

From

From the 15th November to the 21st December, the Board received but one letter from Colonel Goddard, dated the 5th November, by which it only appears, that he was engaged in hostilities with Palagee Pundit, who harrassed his march with 5000 Marratta horse; and, on the same day, Mr. Hastings produced a private letter of the 16th November, from Colonel Goddard to *himself*. The detachment was then at Beersea, 25 cofs, or 50 miles from the Narbudda; his march still interrupted, and his supplies cut off by Palagee Pundit. He says, that he had received friendly letters from Moodajee Boosla, but that it was plain he would rather some agreement was entered into for his security, before the army marched into his territory. An evident mark of distrust.

On the same day, Mr. Hastings produced the copy of a letter from Moodajee Boosla to Colonel Goddard, dated the 23d November, which had been forwarded direct from Nagpore to Calcutta. He lays before Colonel Goddard, in the strongest colours, a detail of the preparations making by the Poonah Government, to oppose his march, and of the dangers and difficulties which he must expect to meet with.* He declines joining him with a body of his troops; observing that it would produce no good effect, but would remove the veil from the business, and leave their designs exposed; that it would destroy the friendship established between him and the Paishwa, and the Nizam-ul-Muluck, Soubah of the Deccan, and expose his dominions to the ravages of the armies of the Deccan and the Paishwa, in Brrar and at the Gauts: Finally, he advises Colonel Goddard to write all these particulars to Calcutta, and

G   wait

---

* These designs and preparations were diverted by the approach of the Bombay expedition. Otherwise it is beyond a doubt, that Colonel Goddard's expedition must have failed.

wait for orders from thence, and until their arrival, to continue on the banks of the Narbudda. In the mean time, he recommends to Colonel Goddard to write an amicable letter to the Paishwa, to desire a safe passage through his dominions to Bombay, with assurances that the march of the detachment had no other object than to strengthen the place against the designs of the French. After this explicit explanation, by the Rajah of Berar, is it questionable, whether Mr. Hastings did not, in every stage of this business, urge and stimulate the people in Bombay, to force on a Marratta war at all events, and to undertake the wild and rash expedition from thence to Poonah, let the event be ever so fatal, for the express purpose of drawing the main force and attention of the Marrattas to that object only, and by that means to secure the march of his own projected detachment in safety, and without molestation. An effect which the defeat of the Bombay army, and the reduction of Pondicherry and Mahè, actually produced. This allegation involves a heavy charge. In the defeat of the Bombay army, the disgraceful condition to which they were reduced, and in the violation of public faith, the Company and the British nation have submitted to an indelible stain on their fame, in every honourable sense, which time will, with difficulty, be scarcely able to obliterate. *

After

* To shew, as well the dreadful opinion conceived of English faith, as the just and amicable disposition of the Poonah Government, an abstract from two letters, written by the Paishwa to Governor Hastings, received in Calcutta on the 7th and 12th December current, referred to in the Appendix, A, No. 4. and 5, will apply also in this place as notes.

FIRST LETTER,
" I call God to witness, that, out of regard to the friendship and
" alliance of the Company, and the English Chiefs, I dismissed
" the French Envoy, without negotiating, or even conversing with
" him.

After producing this copy of a letter from Moodajee Boosla to Colonel Goddard, Mr. Hastings informed the Board, that Moodajee Boosla, notwithstanding all his former assertions, and declarations in his praise and favour,

"him. — I have lately heard, that some of your people (Colonel Leslie) have hostilely possessed themselves of the fort of Calpee, which belongs to this government. This measure is widely removed from the faith of the solemn treaty executed by the English. When the Governor of Bombay, in former times, put on the mask of friendship, for the purposes of deceit, and aided the enemy of this government, regarding you, Sir, as superior to all the other chiefs, I made peace and friendship with you, and these are the fruits produced by this friendship."

"You write, 'that the maintaining of friendship and strict union between our states, is your resolve.' — Is it, in effect, for the preservation of friendship, that you trouble the dominions of this government? — Such a mode of conduct is inconsistent with the maxims and usages of high and illustrious Chiefs. It is mutually incumbent on us, to preserve inviolate the terms of the treaty. Should any deviation arise therein, they are the effects of the will and dispensation of God."

SECOND LETTER.

"It is universally allowed, that there is nothing in the world more excellent than friendship and harmony, which are blessings to mankind in general. The maintenance of every article of the treaty, is equally incumbent on both parties. It is not stipulated in any article of the treaty, that either party may send forces through the dominions of the other, without consulting him beforehand; and cause trouble and distress to the people. To what rule of friendship can be attributed the stationing garrisons in the country of the other party? What has happened, is then agreeable to English faith. — In proof of this assertion, be it observed, that Colonel Leslie has kept with him Roganautrow's vakeel; and, in conjunction with him, collects money from the dominions of this government, by intimidating its subjects. This being the case, what becomes of your assurances before recited?" — After recapitulating many abuses and circumstances, with just reproaches, on the mode of administering the Company's government in Calcutta and Bombay, he concludes thus, — "It *is the dictate of sound policy, that you withdraw your troops into your own territory. This will be a convincing proof of the since-*

rity

favour, was not the real Rajah of Berar, but only the Naib rajah, or deputy, during a minority; and that he was then at the point of death.

Mr. Francis finding that all this important intelligence was not followed by any motion from the Governor, proposed two questions to the Board. " First, That it appeared that Moodajee Boofla was not inclined to join Colonel Goddard —Secondly, That it was Moodajee Boofla's opinion, that the continuance of Colonel Goddard's march would be attended with the greatest difficulties and dangers." The object of these questions appears evident, if they had not been resolved in the negative, by Mr. Haftings and Mr. Barwell, to have been to establish the affirmative, as a ground for recalling the detachment, or sending it along the Narbudda to Baroach.

By Moodajee Boofla's letter of the 23d November, it is singularly manifest, that, on that day, or any day before, he had not entertained even a remote idea of breaking with the Poonah Government; that he was alarmed for the safety of his own country and very determined not to join Colonel Goddard, and unwilling to allow the detachment to enter his country under any pretext. He speaks the language of a man of sense, and he advises and represents facts and apparent circumstances like a candid friend, and a lover of humanity and justice. But his letters discover no appearance of that intrepid firm character, which Mr. Haftings,

" rity of your friendship, and will spread the fame of your good name
" throughout the universe. From the commencement of the govern-
" ment of the Paishwa, they have entered into treaties with many of
" the Chiefs of the East and West, and have never before experien-
" ced such a want of faith, from any one. — Nor ever, to the pre-
" sent time, deviated from their engagements, or been wanting to
" the duties of friendship and alliance. The blame rests with you."

ings, (with delusive enthusiasm seemingly) ascribed to him, in his letter to Divagee Pundit, the Rajah's minister, on the 23d November. "*as a person of approved spirit and bravery,*" on which he (Mr. Hastings) professed to rest his hopes, "*that he would ardently catch at the objects presented to his view.*" And though it may be strictly true, as Mr. Hastings said in the same letter, "*That, in the whole of his own conduct, he had departed from the common line of policy, in making advances, when others in his situation would have waited for solicitations;*"* it does not appear that all his advances, and the flattering object presented to his ambition, have produced either an ardour, or a favourable impression on the mind of Moodajee Boosla.

But if, after all, Moodajee Boosla be not the *real* Rajah of Berar, it remained to be considered, whether the state of Berar could be bound by any act of his; or whether the alliance, offensive and defensive, which Colonel Goddard was directed to form with him in the terms of Mr. Elliot's commission, could be concluded with honour and safety to the Company, when it was previously admitted, that one of the parties had no right in his own person, and the character in which he appeared, to conclude such alliance.

On the 28th December, the Governor moved in council, that two battalions be ordered from the barracks in Calcutta,† under the command of Major Camac, to reinforce Colonel Goddard, in order to supply all losses which the detachment had suffered by Colonel Leslie's

---

* Vide the letter in Appendix, A. No. 1.

† The most distant station of all the Company's garrisons, from the country where Colonel Goddard's army lay. Besides that, the motion had an immediate tendency to weaken and expose the principal fortress and capital, by which the British empire in India hung suspended.

Leslie's delays, and by the length of their march. That they should proceed to the western frontier of Pallamoro, and there wait the directions of Colonel Goddard, either for a junction with him, *for the protection of Moodajee Boosla's capital*, or to preserve the communication with the Company's provinces. Before the question was put, Mr. Francis desired to see the returns of the detachment, that the Board might know what loss it had really suffered, and on what grounds the reinforcement was proposed. But, no return; no letters; no explanations of any kind, were produced. Mr. Barwell declared, " *That there was no indispensible necessity to influence the propositions; and that if he was to form his opinion, simply on the necessity of the thing, he should certainly vote against the march of the troops.*" Mr. Hastings, under colour of an objection urged by Mr. Francis, to the private correspondence carried on between him and the commanding officer, said, " *That he had been thereby discouraged from affording the Board, in their collective capacity, those lights, which upon many points were necessary for their information.*" Let the world judge of a declaration, so daring and bold, from the chief servant of a company of merchants, acting in immediate concert with a council, whose opinions had power to over-rule his own. It will not admit of animadversion, the language being too plain and explicit, as it was expressed.

Other remarks of serious consequences occur upon the proceedings of this day. A reinforcement is ordered, upon a simple presumption that the detachment has suffered a considerable loss. No return, or letters are produced to prove it, and all lights avowedly withheld from the Board. Mr. Barwell, at the same time, " *denies the necessity of the measure.*" And Mr. Hastings himself, in the course of the debate, observes, " *That the loss bears no degree of proportion to the reinforcement,*
" and

"*and has, in effect, been inconsiderable.*" The purpose of this reinforcement must therefore be, to provide for the protection of Nagpore, the capital of Berar; or, as Mr. Barwell expressed it, "*to give that security to the possessions of the Berar Chief, as to dispel every apprehension he may entertain of the hostilities with which he may be threatened.*" From these explanations, it is to be understood, that the Rajah of Berar, who with the assistance of the detachment, was to overset the Marratta state, and to invade the dominions of the Deccan Soubah, wants, now, two battalions of the Company's sepoys for the protection of his own capital, and the security of his dominions.

December 31, 1778. In consequence of the resolution of reinforcing Colonel Goddard's detachment, the Governor moved, upon the 31st December, in council, that although two battalions of sepoys were more than equal to the losses sustained by the detachment, yet as it may be adviseable to guard against *all possible* contingencies, which it may not be so easy to provide for in future, he therefore proposed that 700 rank and file, sepoys, *without officers or arms*, be added to Major Camac's two battalions; and that in this *unarmed* and *unofficered* state, unaccompanied by any escort, through a long and hazardous country, to join Major Camac at Bissnepore, from the Presidency, Midapore, and Barampore.*

Mr. Francis opposed the measure, by a nervous, pithy minute, in which he was supported by Mr. Wheler. He censured as well the unmilitary and dangerous expedient, as the addition altogether. The majority, at length,

* The first advance to Major Camac, to defray the charge of this reinforcement, was 436,793 current rupees, equal to 43,680 l. sterling.

length, yielded to the reasons urged against the unarmed and unofficered march, and contented, that they march *with arms.*

On the 4th January, 1779, Mr Hastings informed the Board, that by a letter from Colonel Goddard, dated the 30th November, the detachment was arrived on the banks of the Narbudda, after a fatiguing march through difficult passes in the mountains, and that he then saw no impediment to his crossing the river.

By letters of the 2d and 5th December, communicated by Mr. Hastings on the 7th January, Colonel Goddard informs the Board, that he had crossed the Narbudda, and was encamped on the southern banks of that river, within the territory of Berar, where he waited to be informed of the Rajah's final resolution. He says, "*that all the artillery and gun carriages were* "*much shattered, and in want of repair; but that the num-* "*ber of sick was reduced from* 1000 *to about* 400."

The Governor presented to the Board, a long and interesting letter from Moodajee Boosla, under date the 5th December, which was received in Calcutta the 2d instant. Instead of joining Colonel Goddard, the Rajah gives Mr. Hastings a great deal of good advice, both moral and political, concerning the preservation of peace, fidelity of engagements, justice, clemency, &c. but in particular, "*he recommends it to him to act with* "*deliberation, and to proportion his means to his ends;*" observing, "*that it is a proverb, that whatever is deli-* "*berately done, is done well.*" The letter breathes so much good sense, humanity, justice, and sound doctrine, that in justice to its author, it will obtain a place in the appendix; to which an attentive perusal is recommended, for the satisfaction of the reader.*

On

* Vide Appendix, A. No. 2.

On the whole, it appears clearly, by these letters, that the Rajah of Berar, never had an idea of the nature and extent of Mr. Hastings's views, much less of waging war against the Marratta regency, and the Soubah of the Deccan, or of entering into any engagements with the Company, that could lead him into a rupture with either of these states, his neighbours. Indeed, Mr. Hastings, in his recited letter of 23d November, avows, " *that the suggestion originated solely in himself; that he laid it as a bait to the Rajah's ambition; that without observing the common and necessary rules of policy, he had advanced, unsolicited; and that he had trusted to the Rajah's approved bravery and spirit, to catch ardently at the object, which the Governor's ingenuity and personal friendship had generously designed for his aggrandisement.*" The Rajah, wisely preferring peace in mediocrity, to the flattering but uncertain bait thus offered to his ambition, undertook to vindicate the Paishwa from the designs imputed to him by the Company's servants, of a secret connection with the French, and earnestly offers his own mediation to effect a perfect reconciliation, an offer which should immediately have been accepted of. These sentiments in the Rajah, should have been considered as a step towards taking a direct part with his countrymen, if the Company declined to acquiesce in his mediation, which strongly implied a distrust in their faith and honour, as acting under the same insatiable influence.* At all events, he disclaims every thought of joining the Company against the Marrattas. After enumerating the several chiefs, and their forces, who were prepared to oppose Colonel Goddard, he expresly says, " *The junction of a body of my forces with Colonel Goddard's, would*

" *avail*

---

* The Rajah, accordingly, joined in the confederacy against the Company, when his offers of mediation were rejected, and he found that the views of Mr. Hastings were apparently hostile to *all* the native states of Hindostan.

" avail nothing in the face of such large armies, but would
" only involve me in the greatest losses; yet neither was it
" adviseable for Colonel Goddard to return, which would di-
" minish the awe and respect in which he was held." In
the end, he tells, "*that the times require, that a concili-
" ation take place with the Poonah ministers.*" Thus all
India beheld the critical situation to which Mr Hastings's politics had precipitated the power, which, when
he entered upon the administration thereof, was vener-
ated and courted by all, except Hyder-Alli-Cawn, who
dreaded it.

* Supposing it possible, that every objection to the
measure, on the score of prudence or expediency, could
be answered or removed, or that any degree of success
should hereafter furnish an unexpected argument in its
defence, there is still another important point of view,
in which it becomes the Company's dignity and wisdom to consider it. When Mr. Hastings engaged the
Company's arms in offensive wars, without necessity or
provocation, when he implicated their government in
treaties and alliances with the Indian powers, of which
war, acquisition, and conquest, are the sole objects;
when he sent their troops far away from the defence of
their own territories, when he disturbed the peace of
India, and when he avowed a vain, ambitious purpose,
so far as to declare, " *If the British arms and influence*
" *have suffered a severe check in the western world, it is*
" *the more incumbent on those who are charged with the in-*
" *terests of Great Britain in the East, to exert themselves*
" *for the retrieval of the national loss. That we have the*
" *means in our power; and that with such superior advan-*
" *tages as we possess over every power which can oppose us,*
" *we*

---

* This paragraph is the just idea of a person who knew the spirit
and effect of the whole projects of the Company's leading servants
in India. It is borrowed, literally.

"*we should not act merely on the defensive.*" Did not Mr. Hastings, by this declaration, subvert the fundamental principles of the Company's policy? Did he not disobey their repeated and most peremptory commands, and transgress every line of limitation which they had prescribed for the administration of their affairs in India? If the affirmative should appear true, the Court of Directors will undoubtedly recall to their remembrance, the principles on which the Rohilla war was unanimously condemned by them, and how grossly their condemnation of that measure has been slighted. They will reflect on the nature and extent of the trust reposed in them by the Company, and by the nation; and seriously consider, on how precarious a foundation, the British empire in India stands, when one daring individual can, at his pleasure, subvert every principle of their government, violate their most positive orders and solemn instructions, contemn their authority, and set their power at defiance. It will not, it is to be hoped, be too late for them to weigh the disgraceful and dangerous consequences of uniting constant condemnation with constant impunity, and of continuing men in stations of the highest trust and dignity, whom, if we may rely on the opinion they have repeatedly expressed of their conduct and character, they ought not to think worthy of the lowest.

January 11, 1779. Mr. Francis, at a Board held the 11th January, delivered a minute to be recorded, in which his sentiments are stated at large, respecting Moodajee Boosla's conduct, and the critical position of the detachment, as well as that clearness of perspicuity and ability, which have distinguished his opposition and general conduct.* In this minute, the contents of the Rajah's letter are strictly canvassed, and a conclusion drawn from them, that recalling the detachment would be

* Vide the minute in Appendix, A. No. 3.

be the most adviseable step in a situation which admits of no one eligible resolution. To this measure, the Governor, as the strongest proof he could exhibit of the unanswerable sentiments and arguments, composedly replied thus: "*I have seen Mr. Francis's minute, and do not think necessary or proper to reply to it.*"

In a day or two after, the Board received the first intelligence, by way of Madras, of the motion of an army from Bombay, to reinstate Roganaut-row in the Regency of Poonah.

January 25. Letters of the 30th December, from Moodajee Boosla, were produced in Council on the 25th January, confirming in the most explicit terms, the declarations he had made some weeks before in his letters to Colonel Goddard and the Governor, still urging the necessity of an accommodation with the Regency of Poonah, and refusing to join the Company against them. On this day, the Governor, notwithstanding his professed resolution, not to answer Mr. Francis's minute of the 11th instant, quoted and reprobated the opinion contained in it, in terms full of passion and contempt. Yet with so many new and material facts before him, with the certain knowledge of Moodajee Boosla's final resolutions, and of the measures taken at Bombay in favour of Roganaut-row, he himself proposed nothing, but left Colonel Goddard without orders or instructions of any kind.

Letters from Bombay of the 12th December, received about the 28th January, advised that their forces, amounting to 3910, officers included, had actually taken the field, to conduct Roganaut-row to Poonah. That they had come to that resolution on the 12th October. That they had concluded a new treaty with Ro-
ganaut-

ganaut-row. That their lateſt intelligence from Europe, gave them not the ſmalleſt apprehenſion of danger to Bombay in the abſence of their troops. That the whole conduct of the expedition, was entruſted to a committee conſiſting of Meſſ Carnac, Egerton, and Moſtyn. That whatever turn affairs might take at Poonah, they ſhould certainly require a conſiderable augmentation of their force to defend their new acquiſitions, and garriſon Bombay. That Mr. Draper diſſented from the whole of the meaſure. And that Hyder-Alli-Cawn continued to ſhew a diſpoſition very favourable to the French. They concluded with requeſting the government of Bengal, immediately to ſend them the annual ſupply. Mr. Haſtings declared his intention of laying ſome propoſitions before the Board, in a few days, in conſequence of the preceding advices from Bombay.

February 1, 1779. By letters from Colonel Goddard, dated the 6th January, communicated on the 1ſt February, it appeared that he was ſtill in the ſame poſition at Huſſanabad, on the banks of the Narbudda, but that he propoſed moving, in a few days, towards Poonah. From an accurate map of the route, the diſtance from Huſſanabad to Poonah, appears to be 470 Engliſh miles. As the Preſidency of Bombay had reſolved on the expedition, ſo early as the 12th October, and the power of commanding the detachment having then, not been countermanded, they were culpable in not ordering matters ſo, that the two armies ſhould appear before Poonah at the ſame time ; when, by a diviſion of the Marratta forces, it is highly probable, that ſucceſs would have attended the Company's arms. But this does not appear to have been any part of Mr. Haſtings's plan ; and the Preſidency of Bombay were ſo confident of ſucceſs, that they were unwilling to ſuffer any others to participate, either in the emoluments or the credit of it.

It

It appeared also, by Colonel Goddard's letter, that soon after crossing the Narbudda, he had deputed Lieutenant Weatherstone to Nagpore, in order to press Moodajee Boosla to conclude the treaty, and immediately to enter upon the execution of it; but without the smallest success. That the Rajah declined entering into any treaty, or taking any active part whatever, till further accounts should arrive from Calcutta. That, to colour this refusal, the Rajah pleaded the part taken by the Council of Bombay, in favour of Roganaut row; and that he solicited, as well as recommended the relinquishing of Roganaut-row, and accepting of terms from the present ministerial party in Poonah. Assuredly the Rajah was justified in resenting the measures pursued in favour of Roganaut-row, so very different from the repeated solemn declarations and assurances by Mr. Hastings to himself, to his Vakeel, and to the Marratta ministers, which is particularly mentioned in a passage of the Rajah's letter of the 5th December to Mr. Hastings himself, in these words, " *That his Vakeel in Calcutta had it from Mr. Hastings's own mouth, that it never was, nor is, designed by the English chiefs, to support Roganaut-row*;" and that on the faith of these reiterated declarations, he had ventured to impress the Regency of Poonah with the same assurances. It is proper, however, to observe that the Rajah had been fixed in a pacific resolution long before it was possible for him to have heard of the movements at Bombay, which was evident by his using the same language on the 23d November to Colonel Goddard, with that on the 30th December to Mr. Hastings, and the army did not move from Bombay until the 22d November. It must, nevertheless, be admitted, that the support thus given to Roganaut-row would naturally confirm the Rajah in his first resolution. It is very evident, that Mr. Hastings amused the people of Bombay by instigating them to support the cause of Roganaut-row,

row, and kept them in total ignorance, as to his views in favour of the Rajah of Berar, and the real deftination of the expedition from Bengal under Colonels Leflie and Goddard, whose orders were in consequence as inconftant as a fhuttle-cock, alternately placed under the authority of the gentlemen in Bombay, or refumed by the Supreme Board, or countermanded from Bombay to Surat, from Surat to Poonah, from Poonah to Berar, &c. in a confufed rotation, evidently calculated to perplex, confound, difappoint, and amufe.— It is not the want of candour alone, but the want of mature deliberation and confequent firmnefs, which conftitute fome of the errors fo confpicuous in Mr. Haftings's political faculties. Colonel Goddard fays, *"That the fchemes of the gentlemen at Bombay, and the active part they have taken in fupport of Rogonaut-row, have deftroyed all hopes of concluding the propofed alliance with the Court of Nagpore, until it fhall be judged expedient by the Supreme Council to direct the former to be relinquifhed, in order to leave room for the entire and free adoption of the latter."*

Whether this was a mere pretence in the Rajah, or not, to excufe his refufal to accede to the propofed alliance, or whether he ever really formed the project attributed to him by Mr. Haftings, of afferting a claim to the Marratta ftate, is much to be queftioned.—Colonel Goddard himfelf took notice *" of the inconfiftency of his labouring fo ftrenuoufly for the intereft of the Paifhwa, with whom he meant foon to engage in hoftilities "* And confidered his anfwer to this queftion, *" as a refinement upon policy, that might almoft lead to fufpect, that he was not altogether ferious, and determined upon the Setterah* expedition."*

By

---

* *Setterah* expedition means the Rajah's acceffion to the fupreme fovereignty of the Marratta ftate, it being the ancient capital and feat of government.

By Mr. Weatherstone's letters from Nagpore to Colonel Goddard, it appears, "That the Government of Berar were determined not to take any active part whatever "with the Company's armies; that they had a thousand ar"guments to oppose to those he urged in favour of the plan "for assuming the dignity of Rauge (or Ram-rajah) of Set"terah, particularly the faith pledged, and the alliance of "friendship they had sworn to, with the present Paishwa; "that their asserting their pretensions to the sovereignty "would meet with numberless oppositions; and that a vic"tory could not be obtained without shedding much blood, "and at the expence of their violating the sacred en"gagements before entered into with them." What a lesson of sound justice and morality, public and private faith, and exemplary virtue, is here set, by men distinguished in Europe under the name of *infidels*, to the representatives of a great *Christian* nation!—How little must the English East India Company feel their own real importance, when their principal servants expose their reputation and credit, to such humiliating reproaches, as every expression thus uttered by the Marratta princes, thrusts a keen dagger into their very vitals. When the force and effect of these declarations are considered, it will rest with Mr. Hastings to satisfy the Company, that his plan, stated in the instructions to Mr. Elliot, and in which he had embarked so deeply, was not built without a foundation. Mr. Weatherstone says, "That it seemed now to be the first wish of the "Court of Berar, to set aside our connection with Roga"naut-row; the supporting of whom," the Dewan said, "he was convinced was highly impolitical, and would, in "the end, be fully proved so. That, that Chief (Ro"ganaut-row) was held in universal abhorrence; and that "the prejudices in the Deccan against him would not easily, "if ever, be removed." The remainder of Mr. Weatherstone's letter contained many particulars that deserve the attention of the Company; especially a clear explanation

nation of the views, principles, and policy of the Court of Nagpore; of all which the Governor-general does not appear to have had any precise information, or any accurate idea. To think otherwise would be to think him guilty of the blackest treachery.

February 1, 1779. All the preceding letters having been again read in Council, upon the first of February, the Governor said, that he had not had time to prepare the propositions which he intended to lay before the Board. His intentions, whatever they may have been, had not yet transpired; but no orders from the Presidency, could now reach Colonel Goddard in time, to affect the motions of the detachment; because, if he had marched on the twelfth of January, and met with no material obstruction, he ought to be at Poonah, before any letter written at this time could overtake him. The Board had no other knowledge of the difficulties and opposition, which he might, in all likelihood encounter, than what was to be collected from the Rajah's letters. The Board were equally uninformed of the actual strength and condition of the detachment. On these points, the Governor continued to observe a profound silence. It may be concluded, however, from the resolution to send two battalions, with a draught of 700 additional recruits, to reinforce the detachment, that it must have suffered considerably by sickness or desertion. It was known, that Captain Wray's regiment of cavalry, was totally ruined; and that he and several other officers had obtained leave, under one pretence or other, to return to Bengal.—Colonel Goddard's public orders of the first of November, accidentally produced at the Board of Ordnance by Colonel Pearce, begins with declaring, " *that the* " *unmilitary and unexampled spirit of disaffection to the* " *service, which had so manifestly displayed itself in* " *the frequent desertions from the corps of Cavalry* " *and*

"*and Infantry within a few days, was become a mat-*
"*ter of the moſt ſerious and important conſideration.*"
There can be no doubt, but that his numbers were
greatly reduced; nor was there a chance of his being
joined by the re-inforcement under Major Camac.

On the fourth of February, Mr. Haſtings laid before
the Council, the draughts of letters by way of *new* inſtructions to Colonel Goddard, and *new* reſolutions,
founded on the late advices from Bombay.—The form
in which theſe voluminous papers were drawn up,
ſeemed more than commonly looſe, confuſed, and intricate.—Whether they were intended to be ſo, or
whether they were haſtily thrown together, without
any ſort of conſideration or advice, may be equally
doubted.—Mr. Haſtings's firſt general object was to
heap as much cenſure as poſſible on the Preſidency of
Bombay, as well for what they have themſelves done,
as for the obſtacles they have thrown in the way of his
negociations with Moodajee Booſla.—His ſecond object plainly appeared to be, to break the treaty they
had concluded with Roganaut-row, although certainly
warranted by the ſeveral letters of the eighteenth of
March and eighteenth of Auguſt laſt, which he con-
feſſed; and to revert, if poſſible, to his favourite alliance with Moodajee Booſla.—The introduction, or preamble to the draught intended for the Preſidency of
Bombay, was the firſt, although an indirect communication of Mr. Haſtings's plan in favour of Moodajee Booſla, to that Preſidency, and the language is
truly original, but very conſiſtent with its author.—
He ſays, "*It had formerly been a matter of great concern
" to us, that you had ſuffered ſo many opportunities to eſ-
" cape, ſince the concluſion of the plan which you had form-
" ed in December* 1777, *without taking any effectual means
" to carry it into execution. It now affords us equal con-
" cern and mortification, that you have precipitately undertaken*

" *taken it, after having given us every reason to conclude,*
" *that you had abandoned it altogether, and compelled us*
" *to adopt other measures, which in consequence of your ope-*
" *rations, have been abruptly broken off, without intima-*
" *ting your design to us, and affording us time to suspend*
" *the course of our measures, or to accommodate them to*
" *yours.*"—Let these assertions, thus boldly committed on the Company's records, be compared with the authentic facts already stated; and the injustice offered to the Gentlemen of Bombay, will appear too conspicuous to be refuted. By the uniform tenor of Mr. Hastings's minutes, and the letters from and to the Rajah of Berar, it is unquestionably evident, that an alliance with the Rajah, and an embassy to solicit him to become a candidate for the Sovereignty of the Marratta Empire, were the real objects of that expedition, from the beginning, although he injudiciously concealed them, and countenanced another, in direct opposition to it.—How cruel and unjust, therefore, were these contradictory charges and censures, and the absurd reasons assigned for a change of measures.

To accomplish his designs, Mr. Hastings proposed that Colonel Goddard, (whose march to Poonah he now approved, although not strictly justifiable under the last orders of the 23d of November) should continue to hold his command, independent of the Government of Bombay.*—That Colonel Goddard may demand *reinforcements* from that Presidency, which he was sent originally to *reinforce*; but these not to be com-

* To judge from appearances, it is doubtful whether the Governor's *private* orders, did not, by the same messenger, always supercede the *public* ones of the board. Colonel Leslie's letters do more than justify this suspicion.

commanded by any officer superior in rank to his own;* that Colonel Goddard shall be appointed the Minister of the Supreme Government at the Court of Poonah, independent of the Presidency of Bombay; that he shall in his ministerial capacity, demand of Roganaut-row, a re-imbursement of the expences of the expedition, at two lacks of rupees each month from the first of June 1778, in addition to the two and half lacks, stipulated in the Bombay treaty, in full for the expences of the army.— That in case of refusal, he shall either return to Berar, or retire to the lands *ceded* to the Company, which were (it would seem) to be kept, notwithstanding the treaty, whereby they were ceded was to be annulled; that the Presidency of Bombay shall be peremptorily required and commanded, in such case, to recall their troops from Poonah, and from the Marratta dominions. That the instructions already given to Colonel Goddard, do remain in full force. And that he be directed to resume the negociations with the Government of Berar, and to treat with it, on the grounds of these instructions, whenever an occasion shall offer to execute them, consistently with the foregoing resolutions.

The chapter of this day, may with propriety be closed with an abstract from the preamble of the letter proposed to be written to Colonel Goddard, and a short stricture upon it.

" *We are much concerned that Moodajee Boosla should*
" *so much distrust you, as to suppose, that any engagement*
" *formed by the President and Council of Bombay could ope-*
" rate

---

* This passage accounts in explicit terms for the *secret* correspondence, the resentment expressed at the reprobation thereof, and also for the destination of the detachment at last to Surat, instead of Bombay.

" rate to those made by our authority with him, and there-
" fore decline to enter into the proposed negociation: For, if
" you had concluded a treaty with him, it would have been
" our duty to support it, in preference to any made at Bom-
" bay, that might oppose it."

As the expedition over land was planned and resolved on the 23d of February 1778, and by the 6th article of the instructions to the Presidency of Bombay, to treat *conclusively* and *effectually* with Roganaut-row, which have never been revoked, bearing date the 18th of the ensuing month of March, the Supreme Council were solemnly bound and implicated to perform every condition, which any such treaty might contain, unless violation of faith, and premeditated deception were intended from the beginning.—Why were not the Government of Bombay, in so long an interval of time, and after such a series of warm discussion on the measures in agitation, commanded to forbear entering into any treaty with Roganaut-row, the moment that the negociation with Moodajee Boosla was resolved; and to forbear the commission of overt hostilities against the Marrattas, unless in defence, until expressly authorised by the Supreme Council, or Court of Directors? or, why were they not confidentially intrusted with the design in favour of Moodajee Boosla, and directed to contribute to its success, when it was in an advanced stage for action.

At a consultation held the 8th of February, Mr. Francis and Mr. Wheler delivered their opinions at large, on the Governor's propositions of the 4th instant.—Their minutes will not admit of being abstracted, without deviating from the justice and commendation, which strength of judgment and reason claim therefore, with a reference to the minutes themselves, which leaves neither fact nor argument in Mr.

Hastings's

Hastings's propositions unrefuted, let it suffice, in the mean time, to state the general principles on which they were opposed.*

1st. It is taken as a point granted in the Governor's own terms, that the treaty with Roganaut-row is warranted by instructions from the Supreme Council. That it has received the firmest and fullest ratification that could be given to it, by the contracting parties, and

* Some of Mr. Francis's sentiments are conceived in a language so exquisitely just and honourable, that they command particular observation. He said: —

"The line of conduct which I have invariably pursued, with respect to the late political measures of this Government, and of the Presidency of Bombay, not only exempt me from all responsibility for the consequences of them, but from any obligation of deciding upon the respective merits of their proceedings and ours. That question lies strictly between the present majority of this Board and the Presidency of Bombay. I shall enter into it no farther than I am compelled to do by the propositions before us, and not by the existing state of facts. ——

"In the consideration of every measure which I have recommended or opposed, my original and constant object was " *to preserve the peace of India; to adhere faithfully to our treaty with the Paishwa; and not to suffer the Company's arms to be engaged either on this side of India, by the Presidency of India, or by the Presidency of Bombay, in such schemes of conquest and ambition.*" In adhering to these principles, I believe I have been guided by the dictates of sound policy and right reason, as I assuredly have been by the Company's fundamental maxims, and by their positive and repeated commands. I have it too from an authority which, in the scale of any argument of mine, must be deemed particularly weighty; That in the Company's concerns with their neighbours and allies, the most scrupulous observance of their public engagements, and of the rights of others, ought to be their first and ruling object; for every prince and state, whose possessions may stand within the reach of the Company's ambition, is naturally led to apply to their own interests, the treatment which they see others receive from the Company and their dependents."

Towards the conclusion of this judicious, and indeed unanswerable minute, he observed, " That the expence of Colonel Goddard's

and that it therefore, cannot admit, either of amendment or addition.

2d It is contended that the additional demand to be made by Colonel Goddard is unjust, and can never be admitted by Roganaut-row; and that even, were it granted, it would not amount to a reimbursement of our actual expence.

3d. That the conditional orders prescribed to Colonel Goddard, and to the Presidency of Bombay, in case of a refusal, are equivalent to a formal renunciation of the treaty.

4th. That the independent command, pretended to be vested in Colonel Goddard, while he co-operates with the Presidency at Bombay, and acts on the same ground with their army, is highly dangerous in itself, and cannot take effect without subverting the fundamental principles of military discipline and subordination.

5th. That a junction of the two detachments, which the instructions positively preclude, may, in some cases, be essential to their mutual safety; and in many cases, necessary to the success of their operations.

6th. That the vesting Colonel Goddard with separate powers from the Supreme Board, to treat with the

" Goddard's detachment commenced (in effect) in March 1778,
" and the whole was accumulating in April, as a fixed expence of
" two lacks and 60,000 rupees *per* month, besides *extra* and con-
" tingent charges, besides the Nabob of Oude's cavalry, and besides
" Major Camac's detachment of 64,600 rupees *per* month."

His observation on the 8th article of the Governor's propositions, concerning the breach of public faith, and the character which these transactions is likely to affix on the British name in India, call forth the attention of the Company and the Nation.

the court of Poonah, independent of the Presidency of Bombay, tends to reduce the credit and influence of that Presidency, for no adequate or avowed object; and that it stands in direct contradiction to the Company's express orders given on occasion of the separate powers delegated to Colonel Upton, in the general letter of 7th February 1777, paragraphs 21 to 24.

7th. That an attempt to renew the negociation with Moodajee Boosla, besides all former objections to the measure, is not warranted by the experience the board has had of his disposition and character, or by the treatment already received from him; nor can it be reconciled to the late treaty with Roganaut-row.

In the face of these, and many other arguments, the Governor's propositions were voted by himself and Mr. Barwell, *without deigning a reply.*

The Governor guided by secret motives, pursues the same line of inconsistency, in a letter laid before the Board, on the 9th of February, prepared by himself, for Moodajee Boosla, containing some remarkable passages. He *laments* rather than *complains,* of the *distrust* entertained by the Rajah; and declares, that had he accepted of the terms *offered* to him by Colonel Goddard, and concluded a treaty with the Government of Bengal, he (Mr. H.) should have held the obligation of it, superior to that of any engagement formed by the Government of Bombay; and should have thought it his duty to have maintained it, &c. "*against every con-* "*sideration, even of the most valuable interests and safety of* "*the English possessions intrusted to his charge.*"* At the same

---

* This is a truth of which Mr. Hastings frequently exhibited manifest proofs. It surpasses, however, the bitterest accusations of his adversaries, and exposes views and purposes totally inconsistent with duty and fidelity.

same-time, however, he reminds him, that the original intention of sending an English army from the eastern to the western side of India, was to assist the Government of Bombay in the accomplishment of a plan concerted with the actual rulers of the Marratta state.* He might with greater propriety have added, " *and to* " *excite dread and jealousy in the minds of all the Princes of* " *Hindostan.*" He concluded, with professing, that his disposition and wishes remain the same; that nothing is yet lost, and that he desired to be yet guided by the Rajah's inclinations.†

In consultation on the 11th of February, the Governor replied to Mr. Francis's minute of the 8th, although the propositions to which it alluded, were then voted by himself, and Mr. Barwell, without deigning a reply.

The only subject in the proceedings of this and the following day in council, consisted in the discussion of former points, and cavilling upon words. Whether Mr. Francis's assertion in his minute of the 8th, that Mr. Elliot's embassy to negociate with Moodajee Boosla, " *became the main and sole object of the expedition under Co-* " *lonel Leslie.*" With his usual address, Mr. Hastings laboured to contradict himself, and maintain that the expedition had other objects more immediately in view. But his opponent, by recurring only to recorded facts, issuing from the pen of Mr. Hastings himself, without a breach of good manners, or betraying any personality or resentment, supported his original allegation, and stripped his adversary of the flimsy mask in which he again meant to impose upon the understanding of mankind, as he seems to have successfully done on the credulous minds of his employers.

* This was the first time he intimated the Bombay plan to the Rajah. On the contrary, he cautiously laboured to conceal it from his knowledge, and repeatedly denied every purpose in favour of Roganaut-row.

† It would be improper in this place, not to insert as a note, a most curious passage in the Governor's letter to Moodajee Boosla.

"To

One quotation on each side will serve as a specimen of the whole controversy, there having been nothing new argued, except such illustrations by Mr. Hastings, as the heat of argument extracted unguardedly from him in his own disfavour; and therefore the specimen now selected shall be the most favourable to him.

The Governor's quotation is thus introduced. 'To 'so pointed a denial of the Governor's assertions, the best 'argument which he can propose will be a reference to Mr. 'Elliot's instructions, in which he is directed to suspend his 'negociations with Moodajee Boosla, on the information of 'any engagement actually concluded by the Presidency of 'Bombay, and to conform to it.' *

Which

" To you, I had *unreservedly* committed all my views, *partly* and *indistinctly* by letters, but very *fully* in repeated conversations with your Vakeel Beneram Pundit, as it would have been very improper to have affairs of such delicacy and importance committed to letters, and to the hazards to which these would have been exposed in a long and doubtful journey. *Your caution was still greater, and perhaps more commendable, although I may regret the necessity which prescribed it, for neither your letters, nor the letters of Beneram Pundit, afforded me the least clue, to judge of your sentiments or inclination respecting the particular points of action, which were to form the substance of our projected engagements;* and although from your general professions, and the warmth and sincerity with which these were manifestly dictated, I had every reason to conclude that you approved of them. Yet, without some assurances, common prudence required, that I should not precipitately abandon every other resource, and irrevocably commit the honor and interests of this government in a doubtful measure. Precautions were taken, that nothing should be undertaken by any of the governments dependent on this, which might eventually interfere with those actually concluded with you."

A general reference to the preceding state of authentic facts, is the severest and justest comment that can possibly be made on the above extraordinary style and asseverations, as well the unwarrantable confessions contained in it. The rest of the letter runs in the same inconsistent strain.

* How palpably is this quotation contradicted in the letter of the 9th current, recited in the foregoing page, and in the above note.

Which Mr. Francis's minutes refute by many quotations, and first by a reference to the very passage in Mr. Elliot's instructions, quoted by Mr. Hastings, thus:

'Even the passage quoted by the Governor-general proves, that the junction with Moodajee Boosla was not considered by us as little more than an eventual resource,* but that it was then our main and principal object. On a supposition that the Presidency of Bombay might have entered into engagements with Roganaut-row;' the instructions referred to by the Governor say, "You will so conduct yourself as to conform to their measures, if you can consistently with the prior intention, which you will give to our views; remembering that a defensive alliance with Moodajee Boosla being the permanent object of your commission, you are to suffer no consideration whatever to direct you from that object.'

Mr. Francis, after a multitude of replications and rejoinders, closes the debate by a sur-rejoinder, in the following cool, judicious terms:

'When fundamental maxims of policy are avowedly set aside, the change of circumstances should not only be clear and incontrovertible, but it should be such a one as warrants the adoption of new and opposite principles of action. I am not sufficiently master of the revolutions which have happened in the Marratta empire since April 1771, and which in so short a period are supposed to have produced a total alteration in its circumstances, to enter into that part of the question. Taking the facts as they are stated by the Governor, it seems to me an obvious conclusion, that if it were dangerous to us to unite with the Marrattas, when their empire was entire, and in its full vigor, it 'must

* The Governor in his justifying minute, uses these words, "That the junction with the Rajah of Berar was considered as little more than an eventual resource."

'*must be useless to commit ourselves, by taking any part in their divisions, when their empire is falling to pieces of itself. Either way, our engaging the Company's arms in offensive wars, whether in conjunction with a part, or the whole of the Marratta empire, is indefensible, since it is equally contrary to the Company's solemn and repeated commands.*'

At a consultation held the 25th February, the Governor laid before the Board, a paper received the day before from Madras, containing intelligence of the defeat of the Bombay army near Poonah, which he said, he believed to be but too true, but that he did not think proper to propose any immediate measures to be taken in consequence.

The paper which conveyed this mortifying intelligence, was a literal translation from a letter to the Nabob of Arcot from his Vakeel at the court of Poonah — * It represents the disgrace of the army, and the Company's arms in such humiliating terms, that the probable, or perhaps the possible chance of retrieving the national fame and reputation in India, must be the effect of time, let their successes be ever so quick and great.

The fourth paragraph represents the first conference of the Marratta Chiefs, after the approach of the Bombay army, thus: '*All the Chiefs having met to consult what was to be done in the present state of affairs, they all with one voice agreed, that if Roganaut-row came with his own forces alone, they should receive him, and give him a share of the power as formerly. But since he came with an army of English, who were of a different nation from them, and whose conduct in Sujah-ul-Dowla's country, the Rohilla country, Bengal, and the Carnatic,*
'*they*

---

* See the translation in Appendix, A. No. 4.

' they were well acquainted with, they unanimously deter-
' mined not to receive Roganaut-row, as otherwise, in the
' end, they would be obliged to forsake their religion and be-
' come the slaves of Europeans ; upon this they exchanged
' oaths.'

After relating journally, the proceedings of both armies on the field of Tulicanoon, the Nabob's Vakeel says; ' On the 15th January, the Marratta Surdars (Ge-
' nerals or Chiefs) went to the trenches, and began firing
' again, but it was not answered from the English camp ;
' soon after, Mr. Farmer, (a Gentleman who was some
' time ago at your Highness's court) came from the English
' camp, and the fire of the Marrattas immediately ceased.
' The Marrattas sent for him into the presence,* and Mr.
' Farmer said to them—WE ARE ONLY MERCHANTS.—
' WHEN DISPUTES PREVAILED WITH YOU, ROGANAUT-
' ROW CAME TO US, AND DEMANDED OUR PROTEC-
' TION.—WE THOUGHT HE HAD A RIGHT TO THE GO-
' VERNMENT, AND GAVE HIM OUR ASSISTANCE.—NO-
' THING BUT ILL FORTUNE ATTENDS HIM, AND WE
' HAVE BEEN BROUGHT TO THIS MISERABLE STATE BY
' KEEPING HIM WITH US.—YOU ARE MASTERS TO
' TAKE HIM FROM US.—WE SHALL HENCEFORTH AD-
' HERE TO THE TREATIES THAT HAVE FORMERLY
' TAKEN PLACE BETWEEN US. BE PLEASED TO FOR-
' GIVE WHAT HAS HAPPENED.'

" The Marratta Ministers answered—ROGANAUT-
" ROW IS ONE OF US. WHAT RIGHT COULD YOU HAVE
" TO INTERFERE IN OUR CONCERNS WITH HIM? WE
" NOW DESIRE OF YOU TO GIVE UP SALSETTE AND
" BASSEEN, AND WHAT OTHER COUNTRIES YOU HAVE
" POSSESSED YOURSELVES OF, AS ALSO THE CIRCARS,
" THOSE OF THE PERGUNNAHS OF BAROACH, &c.
" WHICH

* The Eastern term for an audience.

" WHICH YOU HAVE TAKEN IN GUZZERAT. ADHERE
" TO THE TREATY MADE IN THE TIME OF BALAGEE-
" ROW, * AND ASK NOTHING ELSE."

" Mr. Farmer heard this anfwer, and returned to his
" camp. On the 16th, at noon, Mr. Farmer returned,
" and told Scindia, *That he had brought a blank paper,*
" *figned and fealed, which the Marratta Chiefs might fill*
" *up as they pleafed.* Scindia told the Minifters, *That al-*
" *though they had it in their power to make any demands*
" *they pleafed, it would not be adviseable to do it at this*
" *time; for our making large demands would only fow re-*
" *fentment in their hearts, and we had better demand*
" *only what is neceffary. Let Roganaut-row be with us,*
" *and the treaty between us and the Englifh will be ad-*
" *bered to. Let Salfette, and the Pergunnahs in Guzzerat,*
" *be given back to us. Let the Bengal army return back.*
" *For the reft, let us act with them, as is ftipulated in*
" *the treaty with Balagee-row, the jewels mortgaged by*
" *Roganaut-row be reftored, and nothing demanded for them.*
" *Let all thefe articles be wrote out on the paper they have*
" *fent;* which was accordingly done. Mr. Farmer,
" and Lieutenant Stewart, were left as hoftages for
" the ratification and punctual performance of the con-
" ditions ftipulated in the capitulation and treaty.—
" On the 17th, the treaty was returned to the Mar-
" ratta camp, written in Perfian, Marratta, and Eng-
" lifh, *fealed with the Company's feal,* and figned by
" Mr. Carnac, and four officers. After this, the Mar-
" ratta furdars fent them victuals, which they needed
" much. The Englifh marched out, *efcorted* by 2000
" Marratta horfe, but Roganaut-row, not finding a
" lucky hour, did not go to the Marratta camp, but
" will go after twelve o'clock to-morrow."

" Alas! alas! how fallen! how fullied!".

After

* This treaty was made in September, 1761.

After exhibiting such distinguished marks of the moderation of the Marratta Regency, on an occasion so remarkably favourable to their views and gratifications, it would be unjust not to transfix so honourable and equitable an impression, by a reference to two letters from Siccarum Pundit, Minister of the Marratta Sovereignty, to Mr. Hastings, in his highest capacity of Governor General, received in Calcutta the 7th and 12th December, 1778; together with an extract to the same effect, from Moodajee Boosla, the Rajah of Berar. These communications, which are impregnated with the noblest qualities which the human mind is capable of entertaining, are placed in the Appendix under A. No. 5, 6, and 7.

On this day, Mr. Francis, finding no proposition made by the Governor, moved, that orders be sent to General Stibbert, to put him on his guard, and to hold the troops stationed in Rohilcund, and in Oude, in readiness to march. The motion was opposed by the Governor and Mr. Barwell, as unnecessary and unseasonable. The Governor said, " *he wished it had not been* " *made.*" Yet in the end it was agreed to, with an amendment proposed by Mr. Barwell, which carried the principle of the motion much farther than Mr. Francis intended: *i. e.* " *That the two brigades should be immediately assembled and encamped.*" Mr. Francis stated the evident contradiction contained in the arguments used by the majority, and therefore opposed the motion.

March 1. Letters of the 7th of February, from Madras, and of the 26th of January, from Colonel Goddard, were laid before the Council. That from Madras had the signature of Sir Eyre Coote, with those of the established Presidency, which stated, in strong terms, the fatal consequences likely to attend the disasters at Poonah, particularly to the Government of Madras. They

They say, 'That by one ill-timed and unfortunate enter-
' prize, the reputation of our arms is sullied, ...'
' friendship of the principal Indian States, bu.
' lost for ever; and that too, at a period when w
' gaged in a war, which calls for the exertion of c
' force, and the good-will of every state in alliance w u.'
In the conclusion they recommended, ' to direct the
' retreat of Colonel Goddard through Berar, towards the
' coast of Orixa, and the northern Circars'.

By Colonel Goddard's letter it appeared, that he was uninformed of the event at Poonah; he inclosed a letter of the 11th January, from General Carnac and Colonel Egerton, in which they advise him to proceed either to Baroach or Surat, or to remain on the borders of Berar; but do not advise him to advance towards Poonah.

This advice discovers, that these Gentlemen found out their mistake before the first action with the Marratta army.—And concluded, that if Colonel Goddard continued his march towards Poonah, his army would be cut off or forced to surrender at discretion. He wisely and happily followed the very seasonable advice thus given to him. Himself was of opinion, that a prospect of being able to effect the revolution in favour of Roganautrow, themselves, was the motive for expressing so little anxiety about the arrival of his detachment. The Governor, without proposing any instructions for Colonel Goddard, moved, ' That General Stibbert should be or-
' dered to send the first brigade across the Jumna, and
' to encamp it on the other side.' Mr. Francis expressed at once, his sense of the measure, but desired that the further consideration of it might be put off till the next morning. This was consented to by the Governor, on condition that he might be allowed an opportunity of considering Mr. Francis's objections to the motion, before

fore they were brought into debate at the Board. Mr. Wheler and Mr. Francis concurring in opinion, drew up their reasons in the form of a joint protest, which they sent next morning to the Governor, before the meeting of Council.

March 2. The next day Mr. Hastings began with declaring, ' *That he had not read the joint protest* ;' and delivered in a minute retracting that of yesterday. *—— When this business was over, and no propositions made by the Governor, Mr. Francis moved, ' *That orders be*
' *sent to Colonel Goddard, to retire to Berar, and from*
' *thence toward the coast of Orixa, and the Chicacole Cir-*
' *car ; supposing always that these orders were to reach him*
' *before he quitted his station on the Narbudda.*' The motion was ordered to lie for consideration.

In a debate on the 4th March, upon Mr. Francis's motion of the 2d, it was rejected by the usual majority. The discussed subjects will throw additional lights upon the political views and principles of Mr. Hastings. He objected to the motion for two reasons. 1st ' *Because*
' *he thought it probable that Colonel Goddard had resumed*
' *the negociation with Moodajee Boosla.* 2d. *Because the*
' *proposed route lay through the dominions of the Nizam,*
' *who, it is not to be expected, wou'd consent to their pas-*
' *sage, nor was this a time to furnish him with a pretext*
' *for open hostilities against us.*' Yet the negociation which Colonel Goddard is supposed to have resumed, and which Mr. Hastings thinks it unsafe to interrupt, has the invasion of the Nizam's dominions for one of its principal objects. Did not the same reasons apply more strongly and directly, to the march of the same detachment through the Marratta dominions?—It will appear from the Governor's minute, that conquest and
extent

---

* The minutes on both sides deserve the attention of the Court of Directors.

extent of dominion, were held out as his professed and avowed objects, and that Mr. Francis's endeavouring to confine the Company's arms within their own actual possessions, is construed as prescribing narrow limits to their Government.

On the 8th of March, Mr. Francis recorded a comprehensive and judicious minute, in reply to the objections made to his motion, and in refutation of the general doctrine advanced and maintained by Mr. Hastings— the 4th paragraph of which is to the following purpose:

'That the limits he would prescribe to the British Empire in India, is wide enough to answer every wise and profitable purpose. That their arms should be employed in securing what they had acquired. That all their acquisitions may be lost, by endeavouring to extend them. That if opposite maxims are recommended as a wiser policy, they are not supported by the example of Great Britain. That the distant dependencies of Great Britain originated in a spirit of Commerce and Colonization. And, that though their fleets acted with honour in the most distant quarters of the globe, the success of naval enterprizes proved nothing in favour of expeditions by land into the hearts of countries hostile and unknown.' *

Mr. Francis conceiving from indirect expressions, which the Governor had uttered, that the weight of his objection lay to the movement of the detachment into the Chicacole province, proposed again, that it might be ordered into Berar. But he was mistaken; it met the same fate. But whether the arguments used against the second motion can be reconciled to those which were employed against the first, may deserve the consideration of

* The latter part concerning Britain, alludes to Observations and Comparisons in Mr. Hastings's minute.

of the Court of Directors, who have them at large upon their records. In this place, however, it may be material to obferve, that fuppofing any future turn of events, fhould, in the eyes of thofe who judge only by events, render it a fortunate circumftance, that Colonel Goddard fhould have proceeded to Surat, Mr. Haftings will have no merit from that meafure, or from any advantageous confequence which may attend it, fince it has been demonftrated beyond the power of doubt, that its object was diametrically oppofite to fuch an idea. And in this day's debate Mr. Haftings exprefsly faid, *"That he wifhed equally with Mr. Francis, for the return of the detachment to Berar, and equally dreaded to hear of its proceeding to the other coaft."* In the fame debate he obferved, *" that the plan for reftoring Roganaut-row having failed, Colonel Goddard was under exprefs orders, * on receiving advice of fuch conclufion to recur to his negociations with Moodajee Boofla, which necefsarily and unavoidably implied his return to Berar."* Are thefe dark myfterious tranfactions confiftent with Mr. Haftings's public duty? Or, are they either honourable or political?

It will hereafter appear, that Colonel Goddard received thanks and rewards for taking that very ftep, which, according to Mr. Haftings's prefent declaration, muft be contrary to his *exprefs orders*; admitting that he was juftified by the necefsity of his fituation, in proceeding, by forced marches, to Surat, as foon as he had heard of the defeat near Poonah, Mr Haftings has clearly no fh re in the merit of that refolution, or in any good confequences that might have attended it, fince," *according to his exprefs orders, Colonel Goddard ought to have returned to Berar."*

---

* Thefe were private orders, without the knowledge or concurrence of the Board.

March 10. A letter from Colonel Goddard, dated the 5th of February, from Brahmpore, announcing his purpose of marching the next day towards Surat, *in consequence of orders* he had received from the Select Committee of Bombay, was laid before the Board. By the letter of the Bombay Committee, dated 22d January, he is informed that they are not at liberty to give him any precise information as to the reasons of the return of their army, or the probable consequences of it. In pursuance of his resolution Colonel Goddard moved on with his detachment, and arrived at Surat about the 26th of February, having not seen an enemy, nor met with any opposition whatsoever in the march from Brahmpore. — Had the army been commanded by a man of less bravery and activity, the chances were a hundred to one against the success of the expedition. The Marrattas called in all their troops to oppose the Bombay army; and the treaty made with Mr. Carnac lulled them into a security, until it was disavowed in Bombay; and in the mean time, Colonel Goddard pressed his march, and escaped.

The Remarker having, in the preceding detail, endeavoured to shew the origin, principle, and progress of the Marratta war, which cannot fail to lead the mind to understand its probable consequences on the dispositions of the native powers in India against the British name, he thinks it less necessary to pursue the same precision in the few observations that are to follow, in relation to dates and trivial discussions, while he adheres with confidence to real facts, in narrating the leading principles of action.

Mr. Francis, by minute on the 15th March, expressed a concern and surprise, at not having heard from the Presidency of Bombay, concerning the defeat of their army, the nature of the terms stipulated with the regenc gency of Poonah, and their further determination. He insinuated an apprehension, that reduced to an extremity approaching to despair, and having nothing more to lose, they may be impelled by a fertility, which necessity is too ready to engender, to renew the war at all hazards. That past experience had afforded too much reason to justify that suspicion, and therefore, in order to prevent the probability of such injudicious and dangerous measures, he moved,

"*That a letter be immediately written to the Presidency of Bombay, to express the concern and surprise of the Board at the profound silence they have observed to the supreme administration, on the late operations and defeat of their army, and to prohibit them in the most precise and positive terms, and as they will answer the contrary at their peril, from commencing or renewing hostilities against the Marrattas, or any other Indian princes or powers, except in their own immediate defence, without our consent and approbation, first had and obtained.*"

This motion was negatived by Mr. Hastings and Mr. Barwell. And certain it is, that nothing can shew the spirit of opposition, and its fatal influence over every principle of reason, policy, and concern for the Company's interest in general, than the very loose and frivolous reasons opposed to this motion, without disavowing the expediency, and even acknowledging the propriety of it.

On the 17th of March a letter was received from the Presidency of Bombay, dated the 3d February, intimating the failure of the expedition against Poonah, by the defeat of their army, and that they did not think themselves obligated by the conditions of the treaty; but that they had intentions to enter into another treaty with the Marrattas, and had, therefore, ordered Colonel
Goddard's

Goddard's detachment to march to Surat, instead of coming to Bombay.

Mr. Wheler made a long and sensible minute, exposing, without exaggeration, the critical, but above all, the ruinous and expensive state and position of the Company's affairs in India, and earnestly recommended the means of procuring peace, at any rate, in *some* of the quarters, where they are threatened with hostility.

April 5, Sir Eyre Coote having this day taken his seat at the Supreme Board. In consequence of a reconciliation, and a proper understanding, which had been effected between him and the Governor, the latter introduced an elaborate minute, complimentary of the former. And then, after stating the disgrace of the Bombay army, and the nature of the treaty, made on the field of battle, by persons unauthorised to subscribe to such conditions, and without a knowledge of the want of that authority in those who exacted it, he proposed the following conjectures to the consideration of the Board, as a ground to raise real propositions upon.

1st, " That the Marrattas ought to be satisfied with
" the possession of Roganaut row, and to relinquish the
" other terms of the capitulation."*

2d, " That if the Marrattas have insisted on the con-
" ditions, that it is probable the Select Committee have
" refused compliance, and called upon Colonel God-
" dard to aid them in continuing the war."

3d, " That

* This favors more of the style of a *conqueror*, than the *conquered*; consequently it may be thought somewhat indelicate and unseasonable, considering the extreme moderation of the *real conquerors*, on the 15th and 16th January.

3d, "That the Marrattas, knowing the invalidity of
" the act, had evasion in contemplation, in order to re-
" new the war when they should be able to prosecute it
" with surer effect, with the assistance of the French from
" Mauritius.

4th, "That the divisions of the Marrattas have been
" but superficially covered, and not healed. That the
" return of Roganaut-row may excite fresh commotions
" amongst them. That he sees no chance of recovering
" Roganaut-row; but, on the contrary, *that he is lost
" to us for ever*, although it may be no great loss to us,
" except by regretting the wound which the British cre-
" dit has received in the manner of his *separation* from
" us."*

5th, "That the conduct of Moodajee Boosla, since
" his knowledge of this event, manifests the impression
" which it hath generally made on the minds of the peo-
" ple of Hindostan. And they believe that any force
" which we could send against them would prove une-
" qual to their superiority of numbers, and the rapid
" movements of their cavalry." †

Upon these conjectured principles he offered the following propositions, viz.

1st. "That Colonel Goddard be invested with pow-
" ers, as minister, to represent this government at the
" court of Poonah, for the renewal or confirmation of
" the treaty of Poorunder, to relinquish the late conven-
" tion, and not to admit French forces into their dominions,

---

* This conjecture was calculated entirely for renewing the negociation with Moodajee Boosla.

† Artful motives to stimulate a dangerous exertion in the war
against the Marrattas, even at the hazard of leaving the kingdoms
of Bengal, Bahar, and Orixa, destitute and defenceless.

" minions, or to make establishments on their coasts.
" And that the alternative shall amount to a declara-
" tion of war. (With a draught, No. 1.)

2d. " That the first brigade, already ordered to a
" convenient station for crossing the Jumna, be sup-
" plied with ordnance, ammunition, and stores fit for
" the service.

3d. " That Major Camac be ordered back to Co-
" rumba, or to some other convenient station, within,
" or near to our borders, and supplied with ammuni-
" tion, &c.

4th. " That Sir Eyre Coote be requested to issue
" the necessary orders for carrying the preceding reso-
" lutions into execution.

5th. " That a letter be written to the Paishwa and
" his Ministers, on the subject of Colonel Goddard's
" commission. (With a draught, No. 2.)

6th. " That a letter be written to Moodajee Boosla:
" (With a draught, No. 3.)

7th. " That a letter be written to the Presidency of
" Bombay, advising of Colonel Goddard's commission,
" requiring conformity from them, and to prepare for
" service, whether offensive or defensive, in virtue of
" explicit and positive orders from hence.

8th. " That a letter be sent to the Presidency of
" Madras, informing them of our designs. And in
" case of success against Mahè, the forces to remain
" there and at Tellicherry, in order to be ready to
" move, on application, to join the forces at Bombay."

Although

Although the conjectures which lead to these propositions, are liable to animadversion, as well as the propositions themselves; yet as the generality of them, have also an apparent tendency to bring forth an accommodation with the Marrattas, it will be treated with the same degree of indulgence which it received from Mr. Hastings's constant opponents on that subject, referring to the evident spirit disguised in the 1st, 3d, 4th, and 5th conjectures, and in the 1st and 6th propositions. Letters and authorities founded in general upon these propositions, were resolved.

Letters from the Presidency of Bombay, and from Colonel Egerton, having thrown new lights on many transactions, before, at, and after the expedition from thence to Poonah, it appeared, that the majority of the Select Committee are reprehensible in the highest degree, in undertaking so important a measure without previously adjusting terms with Roganaut-row's adherents; in not availing themselves of the power they had vested in them over the Bengal detachment, to co-operate with their own army; in not arriving at a clearer knowledge of the true state of the Poonah Durbar, before they finally resolved upon actual action; in the wilful violation of the Company's positive orders, by the appointment of civil deputies to conduct military operations in the field; in investing civilians with powers incompatible with military service, and subversive of that degree of subordination, which alone can secure a prospect of success; in the enormous quantity of baggage and cattle, so preposterously inconsistent with the distance, and number of troops; in the violation of a convention and capitulation, having, by their own act and investiture in the Field Committee, given the most solemn ratification which the whole board of the Select Committee, and the Company's public and corporate seal, could give; regardless, also, of the critical situation of two gentlemen, who freely yielded themselves as hostages, confiding in the sacred faith of the Company; and the ungenerous manner in which Colonel Egerton and Colonel Cockburn were circumvented, under specious and false pretences, to resign the command of the Bombay army in garrison.

The proceedings on these subjects are voluminous, and therefore would be tedious. However, as nothing can lead to a clearer knowledge of the facts, and the original, as well as the existing principles and views of the ruling parties, than some of these proceedings at both Boards, they shall be selected for that purpose, and the narrative continued by extracts from them, during the discussion of these points, with only occasional remarks.

Extract from a letter from the Select Committee of Bombay, *to the Secret Committee of the Court of* Directors, *dated* 27*th* March, 1779.

Par. 17. ' From the very general information the
' Governor General and Council gave in of their pro-
' jected alliance with Moodajee Boosla, we could not
' form any judgment in what manner this Presidency
' might be affected thereby, *nor did it strike us,* that we
' could receive either injury or benefit from the Rajah
' of Berar, unless he should assert his claim to the Ra-
' jaship of the Marratta empire, to which he had some
' pretensions, and restore the antient form of the Mar-
' ratta government. We did not pretend to judge,
' what advantage a connection with him might afford
' to your Bengal province, to which his country is con-
' tiguous; but so far as we might venture an opinion,
' we conceived them so little liable to danger, that an
' alliance with Moodajee Boosla merely for their secu-
' rity, so far as he could contribute to it, which ap-
' peared

'peared by their letter to be the object of Mr. Elliot's
'deputation, did not seem to be a consideration equi-
'valent to the injury your general interest would sus-
'tain, were we to forego the plan resolved on the 21st
'July.

'Had we been apprized in time that the negociation
'with Moodajee Boosla, was to affect the operations of
'the Bengal detachment, or that in the intended alli-
'ance with him, was comprehended a plan, to supply
'the place of the one originally recommended by us,
'and to answer the same purpose, we certainly would
'not have prosecuted our plan for the restoration of
'Ragoba;* and thereby have avoided the confusion
'inseparable from a complicated scheme, when so great
'a distance lay between the parties. But we appeal to
'you, whether from the letters from Bengal of the 17th
'August and 15th of October, we had any reason to
'entertain such an idea of the negociation with Moo-
'dajee Boosla. On the contrary, in the last of these
'letters, the Governor General, and Council, after they
'knew of the restraint laid on Moraba, and the mem-
'bers of his party, (adherents of Roganaut-row) gave
'us reason to conclude, *that they still depended upon us*
'*for the accomplishment of those grand objects we both had*
'*in view*,† by their giving up the controul over Colo-
'nel Goddard's detachment, whether the plan formed
'in July existed, or whether we had formed any other
'for the same ends, consistently with the terms they
'had presented for their assent.'

The preceding paragraph was accompanied by the minutes of Council, of which the following are select-ed, as peculiarly adapted to the present occasion:

'Minute

* Ragoba and Roganaut-row, is one and the same person.
† The words of the Bengal letter.

' Minute of Governor Hornby, 19th Feb. 1779.

' The schemes of the Governor General and Council, with regard to the Rajah of Berar, being yet unknown to us, it is impossible to found any measure on them. Yet, I cannot help now observing, that if, as has been conjectured, the gentlemen at that Presidency have entertained thoughts of restoring in his person, the ancient Rajah government, the attempt seems likely to be attended with no small difficulty. The powers who are now in possession of the Paishwa domains, together with all the Jaghire-dars, however disunited among themselves, would probably concur in opposing Moodajee Boosla; who, from every thing I have been able to learn, has for some time past taken no part in the Western broils, nor appears to have any party among the leading men in this part of the empire.* And I would wish to submit to the Governor General and Council, whether it might not better answer our views, by supporting a formidable Chief, like Moodajee Scindia, who has already acquired the actual possession of the Paishwa domains, which are the authority of the office, who is backed with the resources of his own Jaghire, and has the person of Roganaut-row at his disposal, to give a colour of law-
' ful

---

* If Moodajee Boosla had actually succeeded. He is a very old and infirm man, tottering upon the verge of eternity. — Can, or could Mr. Hastings insure the future conformity of alliance and correspondence of a series of successors, when wallowing in power and wealth, to the Company? Are there not recent instances to the contrary in every part of India? Might it not, as himself said on a late occasion, prove dangerous to the security of the Company, to unite such great possessions, and of course such wealth and power, in any one neighbouring state; and would it not be highly impolitic, to bring so very powerful a neighbour on the borders of the Company's principal territories in Bengal, as the dominion of Berar would then be in the full possession of the Marratta power and empire.

'ful authority to that he has assumed, than by attempt-
'ing to model the whole state a-new, and to place the
'rule of it in hands of our own chusing; a labour, that
'is perhaps too arduous, and the success certainly du-
'bious.'

The Governor of Bombay subjoined to his declaration the following state of arrangements at Poonah:

'Moodajee Scindia in every change has appeared supreme.

1st. 'Madarow Narrain, Paishwa.

2d. 'Savagee-row (Ragoba's Son) Naib.

3d. 'Scindia and Holker, to act for Savagee-row.

4th. 'Ragoba, to relinquish the government, have a Jaghire, and reside at Jassi.

5th. 'Nana Furnese and Sacaram, to conduct the government as Ministers, and to derive their authority from Scindia and Holker.'

This settlement was passed in writing.—All the Marratta officers were assembled, and told, that this must be looked upon and regarded as a conclusive settlement, and any attempt to oppose it, would be considered as treachery against the state. The usual rejoicings on such occasions were observed.

Governor Hornby, by minute of 30 March, 1779, urges the same language as in the Letter to the Court of Directors of the 27th inst. and his last recited minute of 19th February, with respect to the proceedings of the Supreme Council.—And that Mr. Elliot would have

had

had to encounter very great difficulties and obstacles in the negociation with which he was entrusted, in order to reconcile the measures already adopted at Bombay, with the hearty approbation and concurrence of the Supreme Council, to the other opposite measures of the Supreme Council, at one and the same time.

Mr. Draper, the 3d in the Bombay Councils, upon more wise and accurate principles, declared, "that he "had no opinion of succeeding in any *permanent* alli- "ance with Moodajee Scindia, from the *temporary* na- "ture of his present power. And he recommended, "in preference to all others, a direct and proper ar- "rangement with the Marratta State." *

Mr. Hornby observed further, " that the Governor- " General and Council probably thought, that the com- " munication of another scheme, while that in favour " of Roganaut-row was under consideration, might serve " only to embarrass and produce a diffidence in the Bom- " bay Councils, which might impede the prosecution of " their own measures with the necessary degree of con- " fidence and vigour." †

On the same day, Mr. Hornby recorded another minute, which claims singular attention for the general propriety of the sentiments which it inforces.—Indeed, it proves, that in consenting to the disgraceful expedition under field-deputies, he erred only in judgment. The following passages are literal extracts from it:

" The

---

* This minute merits the attention of the Court of Directors.

† These conjectures are surely not serious:—They carry a strong appearance of irony, however consistent with the conduct of Mr. Hastings, in not communicating his views in favour of Moodajee Boosla, to the Presidency of Bombay. the servants of the same Company, co-operating in the same cause.

"The Bengal detachment must already have cost an immense sum, and its expences, while it remains here, is more than equal to the full amount of all our present revenues. Colonel Goddard has hitherto supplied himself with the sums necessary for the payment of the troops, by drafts on Bengal; but this is a resource that cannot be depended on for longer than eight or ten lacks more at farthest.—The Colonel has likewise already expressed his anxiety, with regard to the burthen his expences may prove to the Bengal treasury; and indeed, if we consider the increased military and naval establishments of that Presidency, on account of the war with France, and the demands which probably have been already made on the Governor General and Council by the Gentlemen of Madras, whose distress for money has, as we have understood, been the cause of their delaying so long, to carry into execution the projected expedition against Mahé. We must consider it as highly probable, that our hopes of supplies of cash from Bengal may fail us.—In 1776, when the Governor General and Council proposed supporting us in a war with the Marratta Ministers, on a prospect of Colonel Upton's negociations proving ineffectual, they advised us, that they had resolved to supply us with ten lacks, which sum seemed all they could allow us to depend upon.—For they insisted that it should be reserved for the purposes of the war only, * and even ordered a separate account of it, that they might be satisfied it was applied to no other.—If this was the case at that time, how much lower must our expectations be at this, when their own occasions, as well as the expences of
"the

---

* This prudent œconomical system, subsisted only during the minority of Mr Hastings. The application of Mr. Hornby was critically seasonable, had not Mr. Hastings acted and thought from principles diametrically opposite. The reproach was severe and just, and confers honour on the author.

" the Prefidency of Madras, muſt be encreaſed much
" beyond what we can venture even to gueſs at. By
" the moſt exact eſtimate I have been able to make, I
" judge that between this time and the 31ſt of October
" next (*ſeven months*) we ſhall have occaſion for about
" fifty lacks, and all our reſources together do not af-
" ford us a proſpect of more than 20 lacks; great part
" of the laſt depending on the clearing of purchaſers
" goods from our warehouſe, and on revenues, a con-
" ſiderable part of which is to be received in kind, will
" be apt to fall ſhort of the eſtimate, while our expen-
" ces are likely to exceed, rather than prove leſs than
" they are rated at.—We might, indeed, by putting a
" total ſtop to our inveſtments, apply about four lacks
" appropriated for the purchaſe of pepper, and the com-
" pletion of the China ſhips cargo, to defray our ordi-
" nary expences; but beſides the inadequate proportion
" of this ſupply to our wants, the remainder will, I be-
" lieve, be thought very deſperate."

" Another very alarming circumſtance calls for our
" conſideration. Colonel Goddard informs us, that one
" half of his Sepoys have refuſed to receive their pay
" for the month of January, unleſs that for the month
" of February is at the ſame time diſcharged; and
" he ſeems to think that this has proceeded from a diſ-
" poſition among the men to return home, if they could
" furniſh themſelves with money enough to bear their
" charges to their own country.— It is true, Colonel
" Goddard is of opinion, that he ſhall be able to put a
" ſtop to this ſpirit, on his return to the camp; but
" we have every reaſon to fear the increaſe of it, ſhould
" the troops remain longer unengaged in ſervice, which
" might divert them from ſuch thoughts."

" Whatever our difficulties may be from the increaſe
" of our expences, and the neceſſity of providing for the
" punctual

(97)

ayment of our troops, yet the defence of
nt abſolutely requires, that we ſhould find
eeping up our preſent force, while things
he ſtate they now are with the Marrattas,
he war with France continues. The only
h this can be effected is, by ſecuring ſuch
nder our own collection, as may be nearly
to our expences ; * and it is abſolutely ne-
ink of taking ſuch meaſures for this pur-
 the diſtreſs we foreſee arrives at ſuch a
o render our efforts ineffectual. —By the
ctober our finances will be utterly ex-
e full amount procured from Bengal ta-
d a large ſum ſtill due. In this ſtate,
ave to ſupport an united attack from the
Marrattas, in what condition ſhall we then
 them ? — Our bond-debt is already in-
 eight lacks. None of the money ex-
Bengal to pay off that before contracted,
d; and to moſt people here it ſeems in-
t the ſubſcription opened at Bengal for
um neceſſary, cannot be filled, or depen-
pon it for ſupplies." †

nd carry his view forward to the month of
t, and imagine what our ſituation muſt
we continue inactive until that time; and
me, whether the moſt unſucceſsful war
            N   ." could

le or ambitious idea, it is to be ſuſpected, ſpurred
his colleagues in council, to the unwarrantable
ut-row, without weighing the ſtate of affairs and
nces, with that wiſe deliberation which became

neſt confeſſion of the decline of the Company's
y one of the oldeſt and moſt ſenſible members of
on; yet Mr. Haſtings urged and ſtimulated the
bay, and the Supreme Council, to involve his
labyrinth of diſtreſs and threatened deſtruction.

" could be attended with more ruinous confequences
" than we are then to expect, without the lofs of a fin-
" gle battle, and in poffeffion ftill of every foot of land
" we at prefent hold. It will then be in vain to talk of
" waiting for orders, or affiftance of any fort from a-
" broad, when all our hopes at home fail us, and the
" moment of providing for our neceffities is paft. The
" Poonah Durbar will foon find the terms of the con-
" vention, which they ftill infift on, will be every day
" lefs in our power to refufe. And we may depend that
" with fuch a claim on us, which they ftill keep up, they
" mean to enforce it, whenever the opportunity may
" feem favourable. After allowing for ten lacks more
" on Bengal, between this and next October, which is
" to the full as much as we fhall find bills for, and I
" fear may be more than that government can conve-
" niently fpare us, we muft expect to be at leaft 20 lacks
" more in debt, which is fo large a fum, that I have
" doubts whether we may be even able to borrow it.
" But granting that money is ever fo plentiful, yet we
" have no funds to pay the intereft. And if once it is
" feen that the dreams of inexhauftible wealth from
" Bengal are at an end, that our fupplies from thence
" are ftopped, and our expences more than double our
" annual revenue, our credit muft fail, and we muft
" fix a fhort day for the period of our ability to raife
" money by loans.* The Bengal troops which may
" now give vigour to our operations, by the time I
" allude to, may be quite ufelefs for want of money to
" pay them. Or, if they were to have no caufe of dif-
" fatisfaction on this account, there is reafon to fear
" their numbers will every day diminifh, by their go-
" ing off to their own country; for which they will
" naturally be growing more impatient the longer they
" are kept without employment."

The

---

* However dreadful the impending afpect, reafon confirms it as a natural one.

The foregoing abstract breathes so much candour in plain, unaffected terms, and exhibits a portrait of the Company's affairs, under such high, distinguishing colours, that the mind cannot possibly err in drawing just conclusions, as well from the predetermined measures which led to it, as the imminent evils which the all-powerful hand of Providence can alone avert.

Colonel Egerton, after fruitless endeavours and expostulations in Bombay, appealed by letter dated the 8th March, accompanying a circumstantial state of his case, to the Supreme Council; the nature of Colonel Egerton's complaint will appear in the minutes of Mr. Francis so clearly, that it would be a work of supererogation to abstract them here; but a striking passage concerning the character of Roganaut-row, demands an indispensible place, viz.

" For this reason, and because I thought it conformable to your directions in most respects, I consented to continue granting support to Ragoba, though much against my own inclination, from a conviction that a man blackened with the commission of the most atrocious crimes, would not prove an advantageous or honourable ally; and that no faith could be expected from his most solemn engagements. However, notwithstanding these my rooted principles, the assistance of the Company's forces for conducting him to Poonah, could not at this time be with-held, without a total subversion of the political system, we had so long ago embarked in."

It appears from these abstracts that Mr. Hastings persevered with unpardonable and inexcusable obstinacy in pursuing the plan of alliance with Moodajee Boosla, against every reasonable principle of sound policy, and the force of clear conviction, in four material points.—

First, had the negociation at Berar succeeded, and been carried into effect at Setterah, the measure of restoring the antient Marratta government would be not only impolitic, but madness, threatening the subversion of the Company; and, in a general view, the subversion also of all the native powers of India.—Secondly, the Governor General having had a knowledge of the confinement of Moraba, and the other Marratta chiefs who adhered to Roganaut-row, before the consultation of 12th October 1778, and the instructions transmitted to Bombay, in consequence thereof, the cause of Roganaut-row ceased to wear any longer a propitious aspect, and should, in prudence, have been abandoned upon terms of personal security to him.—Thirdly, having had a perfect knowledge of the infamy and perfidiousness of Roganaut-row, it was highly dishonourable to the Company, dangerous to any confidence which might in future be reposed in him, and productive of disgust and diffidence in the minds of all the states of Hindostan, that the Company's protection, friendship and arms, should be prostituted to the service and exaltation of a man whose vices, dyed in the blood of his own kindred, and indelibly stamped with the foulest treachery, had rendered peculiarly obnoxious and detested throughout Asia.—And fourthly, having had a fixed object in his own head, and concealing it under false and specious pretences from Mr. Francis and Mr. Wheler at the Supreme Board, and from the Select Committee in Bombay, he misled and amused the latter, and excited them to proceed to extremities upon a false ground, and erroneous principles, which candour, ingenuity, and fidelity to his trust, must have inevitably prevented, and by that means have preserved the honour of the Company's arms unsullied, their reputation unimpeached, and their treasures unexhausted.

May 24.

May 24. The possession of Bombay letters and documents, necessarily commanded the interposition, and should have commanded the decisive judgments in certain cases, of the Supreme Council of India.—Mr. Hastings is possessed of abilities and perspicuity which are too distinguished not to discover the miserable situation into which his own measures had plunged the Company, and it became therefore a political principle in him to endeavour, by an appearance of temper, moderation, and condescension, to sooth and lull the quick discerning faculties of those who had steadily opposed his destructive plans from retorting the chief blame upon himself; and by a similar management and address, after loading the Presidency of Bombay with bitter reproaches and censures on the Bengal minutes, to impose silence on them for fear of more serious discoveries to his own dishonor, by writing to themselves in a style and language expressive only of confidence, hopes, concern, and sympathy. Having, to all appearances these objects in contemplation, on the 24th May he presented a minute of enormous extension, with an elaborate preamble of affected candour, exemplary moderation, and unusual condescension; but, now and then tinctured with factious and insidious insinuations, with respect to other members of the board. He proposed various matters to the consideration of the board, arranged under twenty-two heads. On this occasion also, Mr. Hastings reckoned without his host. The addition of Sir Eyre Coote to his forces, did not intimidate, or even slacken, the determined persevering exertions of Mr. Francis and Mr. Wheler.

After thus arranging systematically the catalogue of matter submitted in the Bombay dispatches, Mr. Hastings, desirous of avoiding any scrutiny which might again bring his own conduct more openly into discussion, and probably draw the whole blame upon himself,

attacked

attacked, with indecent violence, the council of Bombay, without producing any specific or direct charge. The unwillingness with which he entered upon this important part of his public duty, will appear evident in the following, among many other similar passages in his minute:

'If the Board shall judge it incumbent on them to enter into so laborious a discussion, I shall submit, though reluctantly, to bear my part in it.—Reluctantly, because it will occupy more of our time, than we can spare from other more substantial objects; and because I foresee that it will lead to altercations among ourselves, it being impossible that we who have but just begun to agree in opinion, as to public measures, should all become of one mind on twenty-two distinct and interesting propositions, and because it would be unavailing and inconclusive.'

It is observable now, that the presence of Sir Eyre Coote had softened Mr. Hastings, from that imperious dictatorial stile, and silent contempt, which marked his former minutes, while his own casting voice decided all points in controversy. In the above specimen there appears a strange inconsistency of argument.—What '*other more substantial objects*,' could come before the Board, than a measure which confessedly threatened ruin to the Company's concerns in Asia? and yet in the fourth line thereafter he declares, that the unsubstantial objects are become very '*interesting*,' which nevertheless, would be '*unavailing and inconclusive*,' if made the subjects of '*laborious discussion*;' thus conscious guilt foresaw, and seemed to anticipate the consequences of the enquiry; it was therefore natural for him to wish to evade it.

Again,

Again, he says—' That to censure or to command,
' is all that we can do, except in one instance;.'* For
' our censures cannot impress restraint, nor our com-
' mendations avert the effects of past misfortunes, or
' preclude the judgment, which awaits the instruments
' of them from higher authority.† Our effectual au-
' thority is limited to political engagements and military
' operations " *undertaken without our previous licence.*" ‡
' The treaty, or convention, or whatever name it may
' bear, which was concluded at Wargaum, certainly
' falls within this description, *and it is in our power if
' we please, to punish the authors of it by a temporary sus-
' pension.* But is it necessary? An act so fatal to the
' interests of the Company, and so disgraceful to the
' reputation of the British nation, cannot fail to excite
' the most rigid scrutiny into the conduct of every
' one concerned in it, and the causes which produced
' it, § by those who have the power both to judge and
' to

---

* A Jesuitical evasion indeed! Command should precede censure, and disobedience authorized dismission.—What more can the Court of Directors inflict? unless the premeditated effect will judicially entitle the injured party to damages.

† Is not the power of suspension deemed an effectual authority, in the mean time? But Mr. Hastings trusted, that if the matter was immediately, and without local investigation, referred home, the superior influence of his own friends, would slur over the enquiry without scrupulous scrutiny, and rest the whole blame upon the Bombay Council; whereas, if the enquiry was investigated in India, he dreaded, that the minutes of those who opposed his measures, and those of the Bombay Council, would trace the subject to its source, and distribute the stigmas among the culprits, according to their respective degrees of criminality.

‡ Here Mr. Hastings has carried affected moderation beyond his purposes, because the Bombay Council having had ' *previous licence,*' he, unguardedly, criminates himself, as the sole author of the licence.

§ By this bravado, he expected to impress the public with an idea of innocence in himself, and to avoid the censure of a direct participation, if not that of appearing the ostensible criminal.

' to punish ; which, perhaps, in this case, *we have not
' in effect*.'*

' The charge preferred by Governor Hornby against
' Colonel Egerton, and Lieutenant Colonel Cockburn,
' and referred expressly to us for our judgment upon
' it, " is but a small portion of a long series of long
" apparent misconduct, every part of which has an
" equal claim, and many greater, to our consideration
" of them." There was no need of this reference to
' us, " nor are we competent to receive it." †

' Mr. Hastings, after bestowing a profusion of re-
' proach, invective and abuse, on the Bombay govern-
' ment, for the whole of their conduct, all at once
' sweetened his tone into a tender melodious accent, and
' he *urged temper in the form of conveying the opinions and*
' *resolutions of the Board to men who were not exempt from*
' *the common infirmities of humanity, in order to give en-*
' *couragement and confidence to their future proceedings, in-*
' *stead of adding to their depression, which, by inflaming*
' *their passions, might prove the surest means of converting*
' *the power still left in their hands into instruments of oppo-*
' *sition, and even of the defeat of the very measures which*
' *required their agency, and could not be accomplished with-*
' *out it*.'

This is the most severe and cruel part of Mr. Hastings's censures, because it ceases to attack their incapacity and want of judgment, but is pointedly directed
to their hearts, and which, in fact, becomes a charge
of

---

* Here he contradicts what he averred but a few lines before, that the Council possessed the power of suspension.

† Knowing, as Mr. Hastings avows, ' those great and repeated
misconducts of a long standing,' how criminal was himself, in
not restraining them, having the power, and considerably more criminal, in extending their power beyond the reach of correction ?

of high, immediate criminality against himself; whether he really entertained those sentiments of the Bombay government or not.—He declares, in explicit terms, ' *That under the influence of passion, he believes them capable of betraying the most sacred trust*;' and although he avows that the Supreme Board have legal power to suspend men of that dangerous disposition from their stations, he prefers the mild and temperate expedient of suppressing every idea of reproach, under pretence of preventing the abuse of an authority, which he, notwithstanding, continues to cloath them with, at the avowed hazard of subverting the whole British power, together with the property and possessions of the English East-India Company in Hindostan.—The artifice and device practised upon this occasion, were too flimsily shaded to conceal the design. The Governor of Bombay erred principally in conveying the power of the whole Board to a committee which accompanied the expedition, and in being too credulous to the assertions of Mr. Mostyn and Mr. Lewis;—but above all, in being too obedient to the dark, mysterious dictates of Mr. Hastings. Mr. Draper, with a penetrating judgment, qualified by experience, opposed the whole measures, in every stage, and was of course blameless;—Mr. Mostyn, whose opinion first misled the rest, was dead;—Colonel Egerton continued under suspension.—And Mr. Carnac alone, remaining as the dreaded and exceptionable character, against whose voice was opposed that of Colonel Goddard, invested with the plenipotentiary and controuling power of the Supreme Council of India;—the Governor concluded with a proposal of a draught of a letter, to be written to the Select Committee of Bombay, agreeably to the mild sympathizing style which he thought most consistent with prudence, than the dangerous consequences of exasperating desperate spirits, by just reproaches.

Sir

Sir Eyre Coote, having prepared a minute, which while it difcovered the animated remains of a veteran, expreffed (in its primitive garb,*, uninfluenced fentiments, and promifed honor to himfelf, and a happy iffue to the truft committed to him, in a two-fold capacity; this performance, whether prompted by vanity, for it contained good things, or want of thought, for Sir Eyre is often abfent in company, he prefented at the board, notwithftanding that he had fome time before, become a convert to the fuperior eloquence and influence of the Governor, and fecond in council. Vanity may be afcribed as a prevailing principle, becaufe the paper was tranfmitted to all parts, as an admirable fpecimen of diftinguifhed abilities, to excite the future expectations of mankind.

The language thus publifhed will enflame the paffions of men againft the author, if by an actual apoftacy from the very fpirit which it breathed, it is difcovered, *that it was but a voice, an artificial found emitted by the mouth, without the concurrence of the heart.*

He entered with judgment into an accurate detail of the whole proceedings, from the adoption of the meafures in July 1778, and inveftigated circumftances and facts deducible from them, to the return of the vanquifhed army, and the fufpenfion of the military commanders in Bombay. He criminated the conduct of the felect committee, in taking away from the military commander the authority and influence which alone could enfure fuccefs and victory, and vefting it in a committee of two civilians, occupying three voices againft a fingle voice of the nominal military commander.—And with juft propriety, he enumerated

againft

---

* He altered parts of it feveral days thereafter.

against Mr. Carnac (who, after the death of Mr. Moſtyn, poſſeſſed abſolute and uncontrouled power over the army) a catalogue of crimes and errors, on which he makes the following very expreſſive interrogations and ſuggeſtions.

'Is there any thing,' ſaid Sir Eyre, 'that we, the
'Supreme Council can do, adequate to ſuch caſe?
'The eyes of the nation are upon us.—Our feelings
'for our country's honour, will be the meaſure of our
'own.—Our powers extend to a removal from their
'ſtations.—Removal from ſtation, ſetting loſs of cha-
'racter out of the queſtion, amounts only to a ceſſa-
'tion of ſalary.—And ſhall a mere ceſſation of ſalary
'be a requital for the facts here ſtated, if they ſhould
'prove true? No! let the acquital or puniſhment,
'ſuch an inveſtigation may bring on, become a na-
'tional object. I propoſe, that a public trial be
'ordered home. Our martial law muſt decide upon
'the merits of the two commanders of the army, or
'ſuch other officers, whoſe conduct upon the expe-
'dition may require elucidating But nothing leſs
'than our national tribunals can acquit or puniſh the
'civil gentlemen engaged in it, who by the exceſſive
'powers they took, preſerved the whole reſponſibility
'to themſelves."

What a pity that theſe ſentiments poſſeſſed his mind, but for a few days only; it will appear by the minutes, that on the 7th and 10th of June he adopted others, directly oppoſite; and on the 14th June ſubſcribed to a letter, which ſacrificed the military Commanders of Bombay to the deciſion of the Civilians, who were their accuſers, and whom he declared ſo late as the 24th of May to have '*preſerved the whole reſponſibility to them-
'ſelves*' In the ſame ſhort ſpace, by a ſtrange infatuation, (for who can account for human infatuation)

he departed from all the patriotic, juſt, and elevated maxims, urged with ſo much energy and military fire, in this minute.

After complimenting Colonel Goddard on his great merit as an officer, Sir Eyre Coote propoſed, that the rank of a Brigadier General by brevet commiſſion be conferred on him, but adds,

'That it is not in the power of the Governor-general and Council, or the Preſidency of Bombay, to appoint him commander in chief of the forces there, or to give him an effective voice in the Select Committee; as Colonel Egerton cannot be looked upon in any other light than Commander in Chief, (tho' prevented from acting as ſuch) until the ſentence of a Court Martial, or the Court of Directors, decide upon the charges laid againſt him. Under theſe circumſtances, I have only to recommend, that the Government of Bombay ſhall give Colonel Goddard a deliberative voice in their committee, and conſult him upon all military and political points; and that we continue to him thoſe powers which he already poſſeſſes from this government, and further inveſt him with ſuch others as may be found neceſſary for carrying on our views.'—In continuation he obſerved, 'That Moodajee Booſla was propoſed, becauſe his elevation will reſtore the old Marratta Government, and thereby ſtrengthen, aggrandize, and unite the Marratta Empire; which very reaſon ſeeming ſo ſtrong with the Council of Bombay,* if no better can be given, will prevent my ever concurring in it. Our real intereſts are to keep theirs divided; always preventing over-growth of power in any of their parties;
'thus

---

* He erred through inattention. The Council of Bombay thought exactly as he did himſelf. And the miſtake led him to oppoſe his new friend Mr. Haſtings, whoſe favourite meaſure it was.

' thus endeavouring to hold the scales in our own
' hands, we remain ourselves in a great degree the
' umpire. This is the truest road to the support of
' our dignity and profit, as well as to the surest means
' of retaining undisturbed, what we now possess.—I
' therefore think, that at present we should not look
' to renew a war, but negotiate with the various Mar-
' ratta interests, an honourable peace, conformably
' to the directions already given Colonel Goddard
' upon that head.

' But if by refusing this they force us to continue
' hostilities, then our utmost vigour should be exerted
' to support our military reputation in this country;
' and by one united effort, put a glorious and speedy
' end to the war. As to the various plans proposed of
' seeking war for plunder, the honor of the nation and
' the Company, inseparable from my own, will never
' permit me to subscribe to it.' *

Mr. Francis's minute upon the same occasion, will bespeak attention without either commendation or preface.—The most striking parts will be presented in his own words, as follow:

' I ought to apprize the Board, that in the following
' minute I have not offered my opinions on the mea-
' sures, which it may be proper for us to adopt here-
' after, for effecting a solid peace on the Marratta coast,
' because I looked on that part of the general subject
' as already provided for, or, at least, disposed of for
' the present, by the powers and instructions which we
                                                ' have

---

* He after several days fashioned and qualified the two last paragraphs to the mind and views of Mr. Hastings. Both continue upon record, as a monument of his good nature, and pliant condescension.

'have given to Colonel Goddard.—My reflections ap-
'ply only to the facts already past, and which I un-
'derstand to be referred generally to us, for our judg-
'ment upon them.'

The Minute of Mr. Francis, viz.

' It is needless at this time to enter into a considera-
' tion of the justice of our quarrel with the Marrratta
' Government, or of the extent and quality of the
' powers under which the Presidency of Bombay have
' acted, in violating the treaty of Poonah. Those ques-
' tions have been sufficiently discussed in the Governor-
' General's minutes and mine, before Sir Eyre Coote's
' arrival.'

' The following observations are confined to the po-
' licy of the measure within itself, and on its own prin-
' ciples, and to the propriety of the means made use of,
' to carry it into execution.'

1st. ' It appears by the Bombay consultations of the
' 10th December 1777, and by their letter to us of
' the 20th January 1778, that they were unanimously
' determined, not to engage in any active enterprize
' in favour of Roganaut-row, unless they were solicited
' thereto, by Saccaram-Moraba, Bucheoba, and Tuc-
' kojee Holker, by a joint application, under their
' hand-writing and sicca's (seals) and that this was a
' condition *sine qua non*.

' Yet on the 1st July following, they resolve to
' march to Poonah, with Roganaut row, without hav-
' ing received any application from the persons above-
' mentioned, or entered into any specific engagements
' whatsoever, with any of the Marratta Chiefs.' After
the expedition had failed, Mr. Hornby says, ' *It was*
' *evident,*

evident, there was not one Chief in the Empire who would draw a sword for Roganaut-row.'—(Minute 9th February 1779) 'It follows therefore that in undertaking to act, without having previously settled terms of co-operation with some of the Marratta Chiefs, they departed from their own fundamental principles, and as far as success depended on such co-operations, they had no right to expect it.

2d. 'It further apears by their proceedings of 12th October 1778, that when they took their resolution in July, they reckoned upon the hopes of assistance from Moraba, Bucheoba, and Holker, with 30,000 horse. Yet in October they determined to carry their plan into execution, when every expectation of such assistance must have failed them, considering the two first of the above Chiefs were then under restraint, and the latter greatly suspected.

3d. 'In July, they appear to have relied on the assistance of Colonel Leslie's detachment, and to have considered the securing a junction with him, as essential to the success of their plan, for which purpose they then sent him orders to march to Zonir.—Yet on the 12th October, while our detachment was still in Bundlecund (the same station which it occupied in July) that is, at so great a distance, that a junction could not possibly have been effected before the February following; they determine to carry their plan forthwith into execution.

4th. 'With these facts before me, I have a right to conclude, that the Select Committee in attempting to march to Poonah, have acted in opposition to their own profest principles. I mean, that whereas at first, and up to the 12th October, they appear to have thought certain conditions necessary, as well to justify

' their engaging in the meafure in queftion, as to infure
' the fuccefs of it; they at laft plunged themfelves into
' the execution of their plan, when every one of thefe
' conditions had failed them.

5th. ' Their ignorance of the real ftate of the Poonah
' Durbar, and of the refpective powers and influence
' of the perfons who compofed it, is a remarkable cir-
' cumftance, and fhould ferve as a future caution to
' the Company, and to this Government, againft truft-
' ing implicitly to any intelligence we may receive from
' that quarter.—While the plan was in agitation, it
' fuited their purpofe to reprefent Nana, as the moft
' powerful, and to us, the moft formidable of all the
' Marratta Chiefs; that he was devoted to the French,
' and had engaged to put them into poffeffion of
' Choul. Whatever his inclinations might be, of
' which we have no better evidence than of the reft; it
' is clear that they were miftaken in their opinion
' of his power.' Mr. Hornby fays, in his minute of
19th February 1779, ' The lead that Scindia has taken
' in the adminiftration, and the condition to which he
' has reduced Nana, to be no more than a creature of
' his, were never thoroughly known, till the facts dif-
' covered themfelves on this occafion; yet they are to
' be traced in Mr. Moftyn's and Mr. Lewis's advices,
' ever fince the revolution effected by Madajee Scin-
' dia's means in June laft, when Nana fled to him.'
On which Mr. Draper obferves—' That he cannot
' enough lament, that we have fo lately become ac-
' quainted with Scindia's being the principal perfon in
' power, notwithftanding the refidence of Meffrs. Mo-
' ftyn and Lewis at Poonah.'

' In the execution of the meafure, the Board, I think,
' will fee fuch errors at the outfet, as might have been
' alone fufficient to defeat it.

1ft. ' Their

1st. 'Their appointment of Field-deputies, under
'the title of a Committee for concerting and conducting
'all military operations. The success of military ope-
'rations, depends upon a unity of command, without
'which there can be neither decision or dispatch. De-
'bate and execution cannot move together —Constant
'experience has shewn the bad effects of Field-deputa-
'tions.—The Company in a former instance severely
'condemned the appointment at Madras on a similar
'service, and no one argument is suggested to shew,
'that such an appointment was necessary on the present
'occasion. If the Select Committee deemed their
'commanding officer unequal to the conduct of an ex-
'pedition of three score miles, they ought not to have
'employed him. To place a civil authority over the
'immediate execution of military operations, might
'create many mischiefs, and could correct none. Mr.
'Hornby himself seems to have entertained the same
'opinion of the measure that I do.—The commission
'given to the Committee required the obedience of all
'the Company's servants, civil and military, yet Mr.
'Hornby in his letter of 23d December, to Mr. Car-
'nac, says, that in his opinion, there can be no necess-
'ity for publishing it, and that the promulgation of
'such a commission might bear the appearance of setting
'up an authority in the very camp, to supersede that
'of the commanding officer, and give ideas among the
'troops, as well as to Colonel Egerton, very diffe-
'rent from those of the Select Committee.'—He con-
fesses, that the words, '*To concert and conduct all mi-*
'*litary operations*, are too comprehensive, that they
'escaped himself at the time the commission passed,
'and he thinks they must have Mr. Carnac also.'

'Considering that the body of the commission itself
'does not exceed a few lines, it seems extraordinary,
'that the essential parts of it should pass unobserved by

P   'those

'those who drew it up. But, whether it escaped those
' gentlemen, or not, Colonel Egerton has sufficiently
' cleared himself from any concern in the measure. Be-
' fore he left Bombay he protested (on the 7th of No-
' vember 1778) against being accompanied by Field-
' deputies. The commission was framed after his de-
' parture, and he protested against its being published
' in the army, as soon as he saw it on the 20th De-
' cember.

2d. ' The immoderate quantity of baggage, and train
' of cattle which attended the army, and which is said
' to have amounted to nineteen thousand, seem to have
' been unnecessary for so short a march, and wholly in-
' consistent with the plan of an expedition, which could
' only have succeeded by rapidity and surprize.

3d. ' The allowing Roganaut-row to move with a
' separate camp, instead of keeping him constantly un-
' der the eyes of the Commander in Chief, seems to me
' a capital mistake, in consequence of which the motions
' of our army were made to depend on those of Roga-
' naut-row, who kept aloof when he thought fit, and
' was left at liberty to negociate with the enemy for
' himself, and in case of a misfortune, betray us to
' them.*

' For these defects in the executive part of the plan,
' I deem the President and Select Committee entirely
' answerable.'

1779, June 7th and 10th, Mr. Francis minuted several paragraphs more, on the subject of the military
opera-

* An event which he attempted to execute. See the Arcot Vakeel's letter to the Nabob, the 9th paragraph, thus. ' Roganaut-
' row sent privately to the Marratta Chief Scindia, telling him that
' if he would attack the English, he would join them with his army.

operations, to the effect of the latter part of the draft of a letter which he proposed in Council, on the 7th June, and debated upon the 16th—therefore to carry on the conformity, the concluding paragraphs of the proposed draft shall be first introduced. He proposed, that in the letter to Bombay, the Board should communicate their disapprobation of the steps taken against the military commanders, thus:

1st. 'That we highly disapprove of the reference
' made to us, to decide on the conduct of Colonel Eger-
' ton and Lieutenant Colonel Cockburn, over whom
' we have no jurisdiction; and that if we were other-
' wise competent to try the charge, the want of *viva*
' *voce* evidence, to be examined upon oath concerning
' many facts necessary to establish the truth of it, would
' be an immediate bar to our proceeding.

2d. 'That the formal charge exhibited by the Presi-
' dent against Messrs. Egerton and Cockburn, for hav-
' ing refused to take charge of conducting the army
' back to Bombay,* ought to have been followed by
' an immediate arrest and trial. It is a question of fact,
' which could only be determined on the spot.

3d. 'That to prefer a charge and refuse a trial, is,
' in our opinion, a proceeding wholly inconsistent with
' justice, and liable to many dangerous consequences.
' A precedent of this nature, if once permitted to pass
' without condemnation, tends in the first instance to
' leave the characters and safety of individuals, at the
' mercy of men in power, and ultimately to weaken
' the hands of Government itself, by destroying that
' confi-

* Although Colonel Cockburn refused to take the charge of conducting the army over tracts and passes, back to Bombay, yet he offered to conduct them forward to Poonah.

' confidence which individuals have been taught to re-
' pose in the justice and good faith of Government, and
' which alone can engage them to act with spirit and
' vigour in the public service.

4th.. ' That the menace held out by the President to
' the officers, against whom he himself had delivered
' a formal charge of disobedience of orders, viz. *That
' if they would not decline all military duty and submit
' their cause to our determination, he would move to sus-
' pend them the service*, is, in our opinion, a high and
' arbitrary proceeding, and calls for the most public and
' solemn condemnation from this Board. That the claim
' of Messrs. Egerton and Cockburn to be tried by a
' court-martial, was a claim of right, and accrued to
' them the moment a specific charge was exhibited against
' them. That any attempt to induce men under a pub-
' lic charge, to wave their right to a public trial, is
' equally inconsistent with the justice and dignity of Go-
' vernment. But that the intention of passing by all
' trial whatsoever, and of proceeding instantly from ac-
' cusation to punishment, as plainly expressed in the
' minute held out by the President, is, in our opinion,
' highly criminal; and that as such we shall think it our
' duty to represent it to our superiors.

5th. ' That admitting that Colonel Egerton and Lieu-
' tenant Colonel Cockburn, whether surprized by the
' menaces of the President, or induced by any other
' motive whatsoever, had at first submitted to the con-
' ditions imposed on them, yet having disavowed or
' retracted such supposed assent, long before the refer-
' ence to this Board was actually made, the advantage
' taken thereof was unjust in itself, and not to be recon-
' ciled to the fair and open purposes of public justice.
' That they were in full time to revert to their original
' right,

' right, and that their claim to it ought not to have
' been denied.'

6th. ' That we are much concerned that so much
' time should have been lost, by a useless and dilatory
' reference to us, of a question which ought to have been
' tried upon the spot, where all the parties and witnes-
' ses were present, and while the recollection of every
' particular was fresh in their minds. That, however,
' the right of Messrs. Egerton and Cockburn to a court-
' martial, is not weakened by this delay; and for this
' reason, as well as because we think that many circum-
' stances relative to the late transactions at Bombay, and
' necessary for the Company's information, can only be
' brought to light by a public trial, we are of opinion,
' that a court-martial should be immediately ordered
' for the trial of Messrs. Egerton and Cockburn, on the
' formal charge preferred against them by the President,
' or such other charges as the President and Committee
' may think proper to prefer against them, for their
' conduct in the course of the expedition.'

But to revert to the proceedings in a regular order—
The consideration of the Governor-general's minute of
the 24th May, being revived, Mr. Francis continued
his observations by a minute, in the following terms:

' It is not possible that any member of this Board can
' be more weary of controversy than I am, or more de-
' sirous to avoid it. When the Board agreed to revert
' to the treaty of Poonah, we, in effect, endeavoured to
' reinstate ourselves in a position from which we never
' should have departed. Without looking back to the
' steps by which that ground was lost, I willingly join-
' ed in the attempt to renew it.[*] I have no doubt that
' peace

[*] Meaning his acquiescence with the Governor's propositions of 5th April last.

' peace may be obtained on the terms of Colonel God-
' dard's present instructions, provided he enters heartily
' into our views ; *provided this Government itself be in
' earnest in pursuit of its present object* ; and provided we
' do not suffer ourselves to be entangled in the despe-
' rate schemes of those who now constitute the Go-
' vernment of Bombay, or thwarted by their opposition.
' *I deem, the re-establishment of peace on the Malabar coast*
' *to be essential, not merely to the prosperity of the India*
' *Company, but to their existence The sum total of the*
' *British interest in India is involved in the question. Let*
' *a war upon that coast be conducted how it may, the dif-*
' *ference between conquest and defeat, in my judgment, is*
' *little more than the delay or acceleration of the ruin of all*
' *our resources; nor is it clear to my apprehension, which*
' *of these two events will soonest produce the effect I expect*
' *equally from both.*'

' Taking the truth of their own representations for
' granted, it is not easy to describe a situation more com-
' pletely destitute of all means of supporting a war than
' that of the Presidency of Bombay ; the annexed ac-
' count shews, that during the last five years they have
' received little less than one hundred and sixteen lacks
' of current rupees,* directly out of the revenues of
' Bengal; yet their bond debt accumulated daily, and
' now amounts to 38 lacks. By the month of October
' (Mr. Hornby says) their finances will be utterly ex-
' hausted. In the interval they will want a supply of
' 30 lacks

* From 30th April 1774 to 1st May 75 19,13,341,
   30th April 1775 to 1st May 76 37,74,615,
   30th April 1776 to 1st May 77 19,50,726,
   30th April 1777 to 1st May 78 19,36,764,
   30th April 1778 to 1st May 79 29,01,235;

      Rupees 115,76,680.

' 30 lacks. Of this sum the President proposes to borrow 20 lacks, but doubts the possibility of raising so large a sum; and if it could be borrowed, he says, they have no funds to pay even interest.

' Colonel Goddard in his last letter of the 25th of April, tells us, that it is impossible in that country, and he fears in its neighbourhood, to find men fit to recruit the vacancies which happened in his battalions, since leaving the Jumna. But Mr. Hornby himself tells us, and we have reason to believe it true, that the Bengal Sepoys will not stay at so great a distance from their native country.—He says, that if they were to have no cause of dissatisfaction on account of their pay, there is reason to fear their numbers will every day diminish, by their going of to their own country.

' Even before the late rupture with the Marrattas, and long before the disaster which attended it, the Presidency of Bombay told us in their letter of the 7th December 1777, that since their late acquisitions it was become very necessary, and they had accordingly recommended it to the Company, to augment the European corps; that notwithstanding they gave every encouragement, it was very difficult to raise good Sepoys on that coast; that it would require so much time to raise and discipline a further number of Sepoys, so as in the least degree to be considered as effective troops, that it would be much better in every respect to send them a reinforcement of disciplined Sepoys, if European troops could not be spared.

" We should do well to consider how long we can maintain a war on such a footing, before we engage in it.—I will not suppose the case of new miscarriages. Let it be admitted that success and conquest are as certain as the most sanguine expectations can imagine; it does not follow,
" that

" that the objects proposed to be obtained by them, are such
" as we ought to aim at in our present circumstances, or that
" victory will pay its own expences.— By extending our
" territorial possessions, we create irreconcileable enmity in
" the minds of those powers, whom we immediately rob of
" their property. We fill every other Indian state with jea-
" lousy and alarm, and the territory we acquire, comes wast-
" ed and depopulated into our hands."

' To defend a new line of frontiers, new military es-
' tablishments must be formed, and those establishments
' must not only be paid for out of the revenues of Ben-
' gal, but the very men who compose them, raised and
' nourished here to supply a service, which we know
' they will take the first opportunity of deserting.

' Such, in my conception, is the situation in which a
' successful war against the Marrattas alone, will place
' us. But if our success, or the apparent prospect of
' it, should compel them to call in the French to their
' assistance, if rather than relinquish their country to us,
' they should resolve to make it the seat of war, let us
' consider in what manner the contest is then to be
' maintained, and to what issue it may lead us. No-
' thing less than the extreme and instant necessity of self-
' preservation, can ever reduce the Marrattas to so des-
' perate a resolution, as that of inviting a European
' army into their country. If once they are intro-
' duced, it may be a difficult task to remove them.
' *The events of war in that case will not be so clearly at our
' command, as they are thought to be at present; and let it
' be remembered, that on these events, if they are forwarded
' by our acts, we shall want only to stake the fate of our
' Empire.*

" The question does not end here: In the present state of
" things, much more than the interest of India may depend
" on

"on the care and œconomy with which we conduct the Com-
"pany's affairs.—— A regular return of wealth from the
"revenues of these provinces is undoubtedly expected at home.
"The nation, now perhaps looks to Bengal, as its last and
"greatest external resource. But if this demand upon us
"from home were not so pressing, and so likely to increase, as
"I think it is, it is time for us to consider, whether there
"be in Great Britain a fundamental force equal to the
"tenure of unbounded acquisition, at this distance from the
"seat of Empire; or whether we are not arrived at a point,
"at which common prudence dictates to us to fix, once for
"all, the limits of our dominion. If my judgment were to
"prevail, it should be our object to contract them."

' These general considerations belong properly to the
' opinion which I mean to give on the principal ques-
' tions before us, and will be found applicable to the
' subject.'

' To avoid a useless debate at the Board, I think the
' first question should be put generally, and decided by
' a majority of votes,—viz.—Whether we shall or shall
' not enter into a discussion and censure of the late trans-
' actions at Bombay? If it be determined in the affir-
' mative, the commander in chief's minute and mine,
' will furnish what I deem sufficient materials for that
' part of our letter. — To these, however, the other
' members of the Board may propose such additions or
' alterations as they shall think proper.'

' The second question, I should think, to be decided
' in the same manner, is, Whether we should declare
' our opinion to the Presidency at Bombay, that Colo-
' nel Egerton and Lieutenant Colonel Cockburn should
' be tried by a court-martial, for the reasons assigned in
' the paragraphs I submitted to the Board on Monday
' last.'

' The

' The remaining queſtions brought before us by the
' Governor General's minute, require more care and
' deliberation than need be given to the condemnation
' of any thing that is paſt.'

' I think we ought, in the firſt place, to decide ge-
' nerally, whether we ſhall or ſhall not ſend any new
' inſtructions to Colonel Goddard, before we hear the
' reſult of thoſe we have already ſent.—My opinion is,
' that we ſhould wait for advices from him, in reply to
' our letters of the 5th of April.'

' With reſpect to the propoſed inſtructions, I am a-
' gainſt our engaging in, or giving our ſanction to, the
' plan of military operations propoſed by Mr. Hornby.'

Firſt. ' For the reaſon aſſigned by the commander
' in chief, in which I intirely concur, and which I beg
' leave to recite in his own words, viz. " As to the
" various plans propoſed of ſeeking war for plunder,
" the honour of the nation and of the Company, inſe-
" parable from his own, would never permit him to
" ſubſcribe to it."

' Secondly. Becauſe, if I thought a war on this or
' any other plan might at a future day be unavoidable,
' ſtill I would not, at the preſent point of time, hold
' out to the Preſidency of Bombay the moſt diſtant idea
' of encouragement and eventual ſupport in the proſe-
' cution of ſuch meaſures, being thoroughly convinced
' from my knowledge and experience of the temper
' that predominates there, it would furniſh them with
' means, of which I fear they might avail themſelves,
' to embarraſs Colonel Goddard's negociations with the
' Poonah Durbar, and to prevent a peace. By plung-
' ing the Company into a war, it is poſſible that a hope
' may be entertained of recovering perſonal credit.

' That

'That instant difficulty may withdraw the Company's
'attention from things already done; and that, in the
'course of events, new questions may arise, in which
'the consideration of former miscarriages and former
'misconduct may be lost.—But these are motives of ac-
'tion which have no relation to the public service, and
'which neither can, nor ought to have any influence
'over our deliberations.

'Thirdly. Because the motive assigned for not cen-
'suring the late transactions with the severity they de-
'serve, viz. *That it would be improper to add to the
'depression of men, by whose agency we must support and
'defend the rights of the Company, and the honor of the
'British nation*, amounts to a declaration or admission,
'that the same agency which has already produced so
'much dishonor and distress, must still be trusted and
'employed in the direction and conduct of the pro-
'posed operations. But to this I can never assent.
'I see no wisdom, nor firmness, nor union, in their
'councils. And I have no reason to believe that their
'disposition is pacific."

'Fourthly. Because I see no ground for apprehen-
'sion, that the Marrattas will renew hostilities with us,
'even for the recovery of the territory ceded to them
'by the convention; provided we are contented to
'stand upon the defensive. They have no general
'principle of union among themselves, but that of
'self-defence. Neither party, however, can now act
'against the other, with effect, before October. In
'that interval a peace may be obtained, *if we, on our
'parts, are heartily inclined to it*. At all events, we
'lose nothing by waiting for the result of Colonel God-
'dard's negociations.—If in addition to his present in-
'structions, it be thought adviseable to impower him
'to gain the friendship of Madajee Scindia, by an
'equitable

' equitable compromise, in lieu of the private engage-
' ments already settled with him, I shall readily agree
' to it, because I think, that with prudent management
' it may be the means of forwarding a general peace,
' without which I would not make any concession.'

' I have heretofore stated my reasons at large for
' objecting to the alliance proposed to be accomplished
' with Moodajee Boosla, by the deputation of Mr.
' Elliot, and Colonel Goddard's subsequent appoint-
' ment to the same commission.—The plan having
' failed, I should be sorry to see it resumed.—*I dread
' the idea of involving our government, which is now
' too great to act on any but simple principles, in a
' labyrinth of Asiatic politics.—Let us be contented with
' what we have. Let us keep the peace; let us leave our
' neighbours to settle their differences among themselves
' without our interposition, and I am thoroughly satisfied,
' that no Indian power will ever molest us.*'

' To these general reasons I cannot add a stronger
' argument than that which the military commander
' in chief's minute has furnished me; he observes,
' *That Moodajee Boosla is proposed, because his elevation
' will restore the old Marratta government, and thereby
' strengthen, aggrandize, and unite the Marratta empire,
' which very reason, if no better can be given, will prevent
' my concurring in it.* Even the Governor-General's
' opinion comes strongly in support of Sir Eyre Coote's
' sentiments and mine on this subject. He thinks,
' *that Moodajee Boosla will wait for proofs of our superi-
' ority, before he will hazard the consequences of a decided
' connection with us.* When that superiority is ob-
' tained, we shall stand in no need of the connection;
' and if our scheme of military operations be not
' practicable with our own force, I agree entirely
' with the Governor-General in thinking, *that we
' shall*

' shall gain nothing by incumbering ourselves with the
' weight of a timid ally.'

' Before we determine, whether we shall send any
' farther supply of money to Bombay, at this time, and
' to what amount, I desire that the Accomptant-Gene-
' ral may lay before us, an account of the sums already
' remitted to that Presidency, for their exclusive service,
' since April, 1778, distinguishing the annual from the
' extra supply. Also, a state of the sums remitted to
' Colonel Goddard, or drawn for by him, since he suc-
' ceeded to the command of the detachment. From
' these accouts, we may be able to judge, how far we
' are bound to comply with any new demands from
' Bombay; how long Colonel Goddard's present funds
' will last; and at what time it may be necessary to make
' him further remittances for the pay of his army. At
' present, I will not consent to send a rupee to Bombay,
' for the purpose of carrying on war, and making
' conquests; nor will I consent to it at any time, but
' under the condition insisted on by the (military) com-
' mander in chief, *that means are taken to prevent the*
' *money falling into hands, which experience has proved will*
' *make so ill a use of it.* A considerable part of the
' money which we sent them last year, to defray their
' necessary expences, has been given to Roganaut-row
' and Scindia, nearly to the amount of 50,000 l. * —
' The truth is, they have dreamed too long of inex-
' hauftible wealth from Bengal. Under the influence
' of this dream, they have embarked in schemes of the
' most dangerous nature, and wasted the Company's
' property with unexampled profusion. It is high time
' that they should be awakened from it.'

The

---

* To Roganaut-row — 4 lacks rupees
   To his officers, at twice - 30,000 rupees } Bombay currency.
   To Scindia's officers - 41,000 ditto.
                               4,71,000

The Governor-general replied to Mr. Francis's minute, in the following laconic terms:

'I am equally anxious with Mr. Francis, to avoid controversy. This sentiment I not only profess, but I will evince it, by refusing to bear my part in it.—This must serve for an excuse, if an excuse is necessary for declining a reply to Mr. Francis's minute, at the same time that I must declare my disagreement, not only with its general tenor, but with many parts of it; which appear to me, not so necessary to arise out of the subjects immediately before the Board, as to the continuation of former debates.'

'The sentiments which have been expressed by the several members of this Board, have led us into a wide field of debate; from which, it is effectually incumbent upon me to endeavour to withdraw our attention to such precise points, as may bring this business to a conclusion.' †

'In my first minute, I enumerated all the points of consideration which were brought before us, by the dispatches lately received from Bombay; leaving it to the choice of the Board which of these we shall reject, and which we should select for the subjects of our instructions to the Presidency of Bombay, and to Colonel Goddard; and I concluded with the proposal of the draft of a letter, to be written to the President and Committee of Bombay; to which, I have since made some very material alterations.'

'I now beg leave to recall the attention of the Board, to the motion which is thus regularly brought before them, and to request that they will be pleased to decide upon it. The letters involve many distinct ques-

† The causes for this arbitrary mode of shutting out debate are too obvious for animadversion.

'tions, which may be determined by an approbation,
' or difapprobation, or an amendment of each paragraph
' taken as a feparate queftion. Perhaps it may be deem-
' ed more expedient to the difpatch of bufinefs, to pro-
' pofe diftinct queftions; and from the fenfe of the
' Board collected, upon thefe to form the letter to
' Bombay, and fuch other inftructions as may depend
' upon them. *I fubmit to this Board, if the other mem-
' bers of this Board shall prefer it.* *

It was refolved that a copy of the Governor-general's draft be delivered to each member, for their opinions on each paragraph.

At a confultation on the 10th of June, Mr. Francis propofed a draft of a letter, as amendments upon that which was propofed by the Governor, and a copy delivered to each member at the laft meeting.

The Governor's draught.	*Mr. Francis's draught.*
1. "We have received your letter of the 4th April, with its inclofures, by the hands of Mr. Horfley."	1. Approved—literally.
2. "We do not think it neceffary to enter on the review of your proceedings, but fhall confine our prefent enquiries to the choice of fuch means as may beft conduce to retrieve their unhappy confequences; leaving the paft to the fcrutiny of a higher	2. "After perufing thefe papers, with the ftricteft and moft deliberate attention, we have determined, not to enter into a particular difcuffion, or cenfure of the meafures which have involved you in your prefent diftreffes. You muft anfwer to a higher and

* This kind of fubmiffion from Mr. Haftings's mouth, or pen, was fo novel, that it commands to be diftinguifhed in Italics.

and more effectual authority."

more effectual authority, for the difficulties to which you have reduced the government intrusted to your care, and for the unexampled dishonour you have brought upon the Company's arms. We leave your conduct in the course of these transactions to be examined at home; as we doubt not, it will be with the utmost severity. If, on our side, it had been possible for us to select any part of your proceedings, either in the plan or execution of the measures, on which we could have bestowed our approbation, we should readily have done it."

3. "We must desire to decline the reference made to us of the charge made by your President against Col. Egerton, and Lieut. Col. Cockburn, as a point on which we have no jurisdiction, and which is cognizable only by your authority; either with the power of suspension immediately, vested in your body by the Court of Di-

3. In Mr. Francis's draft, on the subject of the Governor's third paragraph, was a literal abstract of the propositions made by him on the 7th June.

Sir Eyre Coote proposed some small amendment on the Governor's paragraph.

4. Approved

rectors, or through the regular trial of a court-martial; to which we recommend their being immediately brought, not upon the limited charge given in by the President, which solely points to one part of their conduct, but upon a general charge for misconduct, upon an expedition that has failed."

4. "Having given full powers to Col. Goddard, to negociate and conclude a treaty of peace with the Marratta government, and having no cause to alter the terms which we have prescribed in our instructions for that purpose, we have only to repeat, that we look to the issue of that commission as our primary object, and the termination of all our political views on your side of India, if it shall prove successful."

4. Approved—literally.

5. "But if the ministers shall reject the proposals which we have ordered to be made to them, and shall reduce us to the necessity of defending the rights and interests of the Company

5. "Until we shall be advised by Col. Goddard, of the result of his negociations, in consequence of his present orders, we do not think it adviseable to bind ourselves, even by a

R by

by an open war, we leave a latitude of action to Col. Goddard, under your inftructions, to avail himfelf of the fituation which fortune may prefent to him; and if a war fhould be indifpenfibly continued, it muft alfo reft with him, who is refponfible to us for his conduct, to adopt any part, or the whole of Mr. Hornby's plan, laid down in his minute of 30th March, or not at all, as he may think moft advifeable for promoting the diftrefs of the enemy."

Sir Eyre Coote propofed a trifling amendment on this paragraph.

6. "Should this plan be carried into execution, we require your ftricteft attention to the following cautions:—That your engagements fhall be offenfive, only for the objects of your immediate operations; and in all other re-

conditional determination, to profecute the war on the plan propofed by Mr. Hornby, or on any other. Suppofing that our views and wifhes, which are all directed to an honourable peace; fhould be defeated, it is not from a partial effort on your fide of India alone, that we can form any reafonable expectation of a decifive fuccefs againft the united power of the Marrattas; for in the cafe of war, we muft fuppofe their ftrength to be united againft us. We will not therefore, precipitate a refolution, in the confequence of which, all India may be involved. We fhall wait for advices from Col. Goddard, and be determined by the lights and informations with which he may furnifh us."

6. Comprehended in the laft paragraph, No. 5, upon the general principle of his minute, of obferving a filent refervation until frefh advices were received from Col. Goddard, in confequence of his inftructions of 5th April.

fpects,

spects, purely defensive. That your engagements with the Guicawar's family, shall be made with the chief of it, and with him exclusively. That you shall not assume a mediation between the brothers, or take any part whatever in their domestic disputes, further than to support the party in alliance with the Company, and his possessions against foreign invasion; and that you do not commit the dignity of the Company, or pledge the national faith, in formal treaties with persons of a rank or power, unsuitable to such a distinction."

7. "We are sensible of the attention which you have shewn to our views with the government of Berar, in joining the overtures lately made to Moodajee Boosla, by Colonel Goddard, and in your resolution, to avoid whatever might again interfere with this negociation. We confess, we at this time entertain little hope of his concurring with our designs. He will wait for proofs of our

7. Observed the same silence as in the preceding, on this paragraph also—which of course implied a disapprobation.

our superiority, before he will hazard the consequences of a decided connection with us; and every offer made to him, while he is under the influence of such a policy, will but serve to increase his reserve, as he will naturally construe it, to proceed from the consciousness of our own inability to support ourselves without a foreign assistance; and this is an additional motive for our preferring a scheme of military operations, practicable by our own force, unincumbered with the weight of a timid ally. If, notwithstanding, Moodajee Boosla shall have answered the letters which have been written to him, by a willingness to accept of the proposed alliance, we shall leave it to be concluded under the instructions already given in charge to Colonel Goddard. If, on the contrary, as we expect, he shall directly refuse, or hesitate, or make new references to us, we have, in such case, ordered Colonel Goddard to break off the negociation."

8. "We think ourselves strictly justifiable in refusing to ratify, even the smallest tittle of the treaty, or convention of Worgaum, and we have already intimated our sentiments on this head to Colonel Goddard, and given him our final instructions upon it; but as we had not at that time before us, the separate secret engagement entered into with Madajee Scindia, we could not take it into our consideration, nor judge of the obligation we were under to express our sense of his services, at the instant we disclaimed the acts of the committee, and will not admit of any pretensions founded on those acts, yet they cannot cancel any rights which have their basis in essential and intrinsic benefits reaped by our nation. This right we must acknowledge to be possessed by Madajee Scindia, and must therefore declare, that unless he should have forfeited it by any subsequent act, he is intitled to a full compensation for any disappointment he may suffer by our

8. The same marks of disapprobation, as in the three last paragraphs.

denial

denial of the acts of the committee."

9. "We have therefore instructed Col. Goddard to express the sense in which this government is pleased to regard the services of Madajee Scindia, at Wargaum, by offering him such a gratification as may be afforded him by your government, or for some means which he may possess from the operations of war, in case peace is not concluded, upon the instructions he is already furnished with."

10. If in the event of war, Madajee Scindia shall be disposed to take part with us, we have authorized Colonel Goddard to enter into such engagements with him, as shall not be contrary to any before concluded, and which he may judge most adviseable; making our future security, peace, and an adequate revenue, his chief and indispensible objects, and the grounds of our engagements with him."

9. As above.

10. As above.

11. 'To sum up what we have written, our first desire is to obtain peace on the terms proposed by our instructions to Col. Goddard of 5th April, and it is only in the event of the failure in this design, that we have formed the subsequent instructions, or will allow of their operations.

12. 'The execution of the proposed treaty of peace with the Poonah Ministry, we leave to the sole charge of Colonel Goddard, according to the instructions which we have already given him.

13. "The separate negociation with Madajeee Scindia, bears such a connection with the foregoing, that we have therefore thought it necessary to leave this also to his charge. The negociation and treaty of alliance with Moodajee Boosla, we also leave to the sole management of Col. Goddard, in the authority of his instructions of the 16th November, until the period of their suspension by

11. As above.

12. Approved, literally.

13. Disapproved upon the principles expressed in his draft opposite to the fifth paragraph.

the

the refusal, or such hesitation of Moodajee Boosla, as he shall deem sufficient, to warrant his declaring the negociation suspended. The future renewal of this negociation we reserve to be determined by our express orders, but without revoking the credentials and instructions already granted to Col. Goddard respecting it. In all other negociations, treaties, and plans of military operations, it is our wish so to blend the powers of your government with our own in the direction of them, and in every formal or occasional instrument which they may require for their ratification, as to preserve the credit and distinct responsibility of both, and to make both the pledges for the faithful observance of them. For this purpose we need not recommend that Col. Goddard be consulted, whether his presence, or the nature of the subjects will admit of it, on all measures, which have a relation to our present instructions, as you have already been pleased to allow him a deliberative voice in your councils; and we are happy to find that you are so well satisfied with his conduct, and his ready disposition to assist in the execution of your designs, as to leave us little occasion to lay down a clearer line for the employment of the forces under his command, than that we have already described."

14. "We have directed Colonel Goddard to execute whatever service you shall think it proper to require, which he shall think practicable, and which shall not be contrary to any instructions, or to any existing engagements; a caution which we hope will be unnecessary, but with which we do not think ourselves at liberty to dispense, while the principal responsibility rests with us. And for the same reason, we require that all treaties, which shall be concluded by you in virtue of these instructions, be referred to this Government, for its final sanction, and formal ratification of them, and that a clause be

14. As the foregoing.

S inserted

inserted in every treaty so concluded, to that effect.

15. "We shall heartily join with you in recommending Colonel Goddard to the Court of Directors, for the appointment of commander in chief, at your Presidency, on the first vacancy; and in the intermediate time we think it absolutely necessary in the present distressed situation that the military upon your establishment are reduced to, that he should have the rank given him of Brigadier General, in order to enable him to carry on the public service with more weight and dignity, for which purpose we have granted him a Brevet Commission for the service, in which he is now employed.

We are, &c."

15. Silent.

In conclusion, Mr. Francis observed, "That with " regard to the form and " extent of the charge a-" gainst Colonel Egerton " and Lieutenant Colonel " Cockburn, I have no " objection to the terms " recommended by Sir " Eyre Coote."

It is impossible, without deviating from the common rules of consistency, to pass over the Governor-general's draft without animadversion. It is a perfect masterpiece of artful confusion, containing throughout, a string of ambiguities, contradictions, and unintelligible tautologies, which, if they are not immediately calculated to confound and embarrass the negociator, are certainly meant, in case of error or failure in the execution, to screen the real author from censure, by casting it on Colonel Goddard, and heaping a portion also upon the ponderous mountain already suspended over the Presidency of Bombay. A review and critical comparison of the 5th, 6th, 7th, 8th, 9th, 10th, 11h, and 12th paragraphs, will clearly evince the truth of this assertion. But the 13th and 14th beggar description, and may, without offending the ablest productions of the late *Holy Society*, be adjudged to a conspicuous station among *Jesuitical* performances.—As the unconstitutional and impolitic authorities and instructions which are contained in it, were clearly demonstrated at the Board, by a refutation which did honour to the author,* as well as by another protest by Mr. Francis; it will only be necessary now, to say, that the plenipotentiary powers to Colonel Goddard, independent of, and as an absolute check and controul upon the Governor and Council of Bombay, within the express precincts of their commission and establishment, amount to a total suspension of that government, or that the whole act is, *prima facie*, illegal; that even allowing to Colonel Goddard an assemblage of all the cardinal virtues, with every ability and force of judgment which belong to humanity, the task is too arduous; as it will be found difficult for a man aiming at military glory, and

exposed

* Mr. Horsley's letter to the Board, representing, as well the illegality, as the impolicy and inexpediency of the authority and instructions conveyed in the Governor-general's draft. See the letter on the Company's records.

exposed to the temptations which are peculiar to the chief command of a military expedition in India, joined with an uncontroled political authority, to separate ambitious objects from the immediate, important duties of his high commission.

The Governor-general in a minute, on the 10th June, canvassed the sentiments avowed by Mr. Francis, and expressed in the draft proposed as an amendment on the Governor's. He entered into a long harangue on peace or war with the Marrattas, as an alternative in which there was no latitude; and that the orders to Colonel Goddard prescribed clear and simple conditions. That if a peace follows, matters will continue in, and revert to the same state as they were by the treaty of Poorunder, without the interference of the Supreme Board. But that in case of war, the Company's safety must depend on *instant action*, by seizing particular posts, during the season in which (in his opinion) the Marratta troops could not act, and thus bring distress upon them before they could resist. † That he had *certain* intelligence, ‡ that Madajee Scindia, and his colleague Tuckajee Holkar, and Roganaut-row, have left the capital, and arrived at Barhampore, with a design to invade the Nabob of Oude's dominion. That therefore, whether the Board chuse to credit the report or not, they ought to be guarded against it, and even to prevent it.

That, *for these reasons*, he was against Mr. Francis's draft; because, in case of war, it will bind our hands, while the Marrattas are free, and will leave the Presidency

---

* Extravagant, wild, and chimerical.

† It proved to be *false* intelligence, if there ever was any such. But it was calculated to intimidate the Council into an acquiescence with his hostile views.

dency of Bombay incumbered and oppressed with the weight of that force, on which we depend for success. He said, 'That he never would suffer the object to be 'lost, for which the detachment, now commanded by Co-'lonel Goddard, was first appointed. That it was not to 'assist the designs of the Presidency of Bombay in their exe-'cution, but to support them in the consequences of it, 'though the detachment was for a while diverted from its 'destination, on the supposition, that the designs of that 'Presidency had either wholly failed, or were relinquished. 'Yet it has since reverted to it, and is now precisely in the 'situation, in which it was originally meant to place it. 'I will not say, what would have been the fate of Bom-'bay, had not Colonel Goddard most seasonably arrived for 'its relief.'

Perhaps human confidence has not produced another more daring instance, to impose on the understanding of men, by dint of mere sophistry and bold assertions, than what is contained in the last recital. The answer, regarding the safety of Bombay was simple. Bombay would continue as it is. Colonel Goddard's detachment was on the banks of the Narbudda, long after the defeat of the Bombay army. He continued for some time, after he had heard the event, to negociate with Moodajee Boosla. Had the Marrattas had hostile intentions, equal to the repeated provocations which they received, they had it in their power, easily and effectually, to have cut him off, or force his army to surrender prisoners at discretion, either by the sword or by famine. And it is no less a truth, that a detachment of Sepoys at Surat, could yield no immediate succours or relief to Bombay, if it had been attacked.

The Governor then proceeded to decide upon the questions which were before the Board, upon the

the

the two drafts of a letter to the Prefidency of Bombay, which he predetermined thus, viz.

" He agreed to the 1ft, 2d, 4th, 6th, 9th, 10th, 11th, 13th, 14th, and 15th paragraphs.

" He agreed to the 3d and 5th, with the amendments propofed by Sir Eyre Coote.

" He *never will depart* from the opinions which he expreffed in the 7th and 8th.

" He thinks the 12th a paragraph of no confequence, and may be omitted.

It was refolved by Mr. Haftings, Mr. Barwell, and Sir Eyre Coote's votes, againft thofe of Mr. Francis and Mr. Wheler, in favour of the Governor's draft. A letter was, accordingly, ordered to be engroffed, and that it be referred to Mr. Horfley (who was delegated upon the prefent occafion to reprefent the Prefidency of Bombay) before it is tranfmitted. Mr. Horfley defired leave to take the letter with him, as the length of it, and the variety of fubject it treated, neceffarily rendered him cautious of offering any thing fuddenly for the confideration of the Board; and the more fo, " *as there are feveral parts of it, which he fears will appear to him more detrimental to the public fervice, the longer he confiders them.*"

At a confultation held the 14th of June, at which the Board was complete. The amended draft of the letter to Bombay was read, and after a diffent the queftion was put, and carried for the Governor's amended draft as follows:

Warren

Warren Haſtings,
Richard Barwell,   } Approved.
+ Eyre Coote,

Philip Francis,
Edward Wheler,   } Diſapproved.

And immediately Mr. Francis and Mr. Wheler entered their proteſts, and Mr. Francis delivered the following minute to be recorded.

"I diſſent from, and proteſt againſt the preceding letter, for the following reaſons, in addition to thoſe on which I oppoſed the meaſures now adopted, at the time they were debated."

1ſt. "Becauſe I deem it unbecoming the dignity of the Governor-general and Council, and a moſt unmerited demonſtration of tenderneſs and partiality to the majority of the Select Committee of Bombay, with ſuch evidences of their miſconduct as we have before us, to paſs by the whole of their late proceedings, without the ſmalleſt expreſſion of diſapprobation or concern, as if nothing were in queſtion, but ſome common and trifling occurrence, by which, neither the intereſts of the Company, nor the credit of our arms, had been eſſentially wounded. When the ſeparate opinions of the members of this Board ſhall appear before our ſuperiors, I doubt not, they will think it an extraordinary circumſtance, that no part of the ſpirit which breathes through thoſe opinions, ſhould be preſerved in the Collective Act of Council."

2. 'Be-

* Let this name to the letter in queſtion be compared with the *articulated ſounds*, which are ſuppoſed to have emitted from his mouth, on the 24th of May, and draw an inference.
  Humanum eſt errare --- is a tender apology.

2. 'Because, considering the claim of Colonel E-
'gerton and Lieutenant-Colonel Cockburn to be tried
'by a Court Martial, *as a claim of right*, I think we
'should not have confined our interposition on this
'point to a *cold and languid recommendation of such trial,
'but should have insisted on it's being granted; in terms that
'would admit of no evasion*; much less should we have
'weakened even that recommendation by referring to an al-
'ternative, of which the Select Committee may now avail
'themselves, under colour of our authority.— This, I con-
'ceive, is no time to remind them that they have o-
'ther powers vested in them; that they are at liberty
'to wave all trial, if they think proper, and to punish
'the parties, by an immediate and direct act of power.'

3. 'Because, admitting it to be true, that Messieurs
'Egerton and Cockburn, consented, at first, to relin-
'quish their claim to a public trial, and that they had
'no right to retract such consent, once given, still, I
'think we should not have passed over in silence the
'unwarrantable acts and declarations of the President,
'by which it was extorted from them. They who
'think least favourably of the conduct of these gentle-
'men, should consider how far the precedent may be
'extended, and what security it leaves to the military
'service in general, against the arbitrary acts of a par-
'ty, occasionally prevailing in the Council.'

4. 'Because the several plans of alliance or co-ope-
'rations proposed to be executed with the Guiaca-
'wars, or with Madajee Scindia, or with Moodajee
'Boosla, must be offered and negociated, after we our-
'selves are actually committed, by a declaration, and
'engaged in the prosecution of it. In such circumstances,
'I conceive, we shall treat with all, or any of the
'above-mentioned Chiefs for their assistance, under
'great disadvantages. When once they see us engaged
'in

' in a war, which at all events we must carry on, they
' will either stand aloof, until they see the success of our
' operations, or sell us their assistance on terms which
' we should not yield to in any other situation.

5. ' Because no consideration whatever is given to
' the case of the two gentlemen who remain as hostages
' in the hands of the Marrattas, and whose lives may
' be hazarded by an abrupt declaration of war.

6. ' Because, exclusive of all other reasons already
' urged, against our precipitating the Company into a
' war with the Marrattas, if that extremity can be a-
' voided, by any honourable means, I deem it inconsis-
' tent with the principles of Colonel Goddard's instruc-
' tions of 5th April, in which the re-establishment of
' peace is professed to be an object, to send him orders,
' which leave no room for accommodation, and which
' ought to have accompanied the instructions, *if the
' Board had been originally determined* not to wait for the
' result of his negociations, nor even for an answer to
' our letter. I deem it useless, even in view to a pro-
' secution of the war, since, in all probability, the ad-
' vices we expect from Colonel Goddard may arrive in
' 15 or 20 days, and though a rupture in that interval
' may be forwarded, and all means of reconciliation
' precluded, in consequence of the present orders; our
' troops cannot take the field before September. No
' possible advantages can therefore be taken in conse-
' quence of this precipitation; unless it be thought an
' advantage to denounce war, before we are able to act,
' and to give the enemy the earliest notice of our inten-
' tion to invade their country, as soon as the season
' will permit.'

Lastly. ' I am unable to reconcile it with the opinion
' of every member of the Board, *except the Governor-*
' *general,*

'general, of Mr. Wheler's sentiments and mine, I pre-
' sume no doubt can be formed. Mr. Barwell says,
' *He thinks we should wait for the effect of Colonel Goddard's*
' *negociation for peace.* But, if we now decide the main
' question of peace or war, the information which Mr.
' Barwell thinks we ought to wait for, can be of no
' use to us.'

' The Commander in Chief, in whose sentiments I
' have entirely concurred, declares it to be his opinion,
' *that we should not seek to renew a war, but negociate with*
' *the various Marratta interests an honourable peace.* That
' Colonel Goddard's detachment, considering the state it is now
' in, together with the Bombay troops, are not equal to in-
' sure success in a contest with the united Marratta power.
' Yet it is with this force, and with this force alone,
' that under the present orders we are to commence a
' war, which will assuredly unite the whole power of the
' Marrattas against us. No measures previous to a de-
' claration of war, are taken to divide them, no alliance
' formed, no general plan of operations proposed. In
' short every thing that belongs to deliberation, and
' which ought to prepare, and lead to decision, is left
' to follow it. But if in the outset of the contest, and
' before any measures can be taken to support or co-
' operate with Colonel Goddard, the army under his
' command should be defeated; *and if the consequences*
' *of the defeat should endanger the whole of the Company's*
' *possessions, as the Commander in Chief very justly thinks they*
' *would, on what principle can we justify a resolution, ca-*
' *pable of producing such hazardous consequences, from which,*
' *at the present point of time, no immediate advantage can*
' *be derived,* and to be carried into execution by a force
' which the Commander in Chief thinks is not equal to insure
' success. The terms on which we are to engage in this war
' are very unequal, when the utmost we can expect from a
' victory, is some accession of territory on the Malabar coast,
' and

' and when a defeat may endanger the whole of the Com-
' pany's possessions.'

The letter having been referred to Mr. Hornsley, that gentleman, though a junior servant, yet acting as the representative, by delegation, of the Presidency of Bombay, did equal justice to his truth, and to clear abilities, in representing to the Supreme Board the plain improprieties and illegalities contained in the letters of instructions, &c. to the Presidency of Bombay. The paper will speak more forcibly and honourably for itself, than by abstracting its substance, which will be found on the Company's records in the India House.

By a letter from Colonel Goddard, dated at Surat, the 26th October, 1779, he informed, that the Paishwa's minister had in plain and direct terms declared to him, in the name of his master, that he would not accede to the proposals made by Colonel Goddard, or conclude peace with the English, unless Roganaut-row (who had escaped) was delivered up to him, and Salsette surrendered to the Marratta government. That in consequence of this declaration Colonel Goddard had broke off the negociation, and prepared for war. The Bombay Select Committee, by their letter of 31st October, informed the Board that they had strongly recommended to Colonel Goddard, not to precipitate matters, but to endeavour to gain time, and to defer any declaration until they were in a better condition for an active war.

As was predicted, the whole Marratta race, including the Rajah of Berar, and the Guiacawar Chief, together with Hyder Alli Cawn, and it is credibly suspected the Soubah of the Deccan, and Nudjiff Cawn, had entered into a close combination, and confederacy, to reduce the British empire in India, and that they are carrying on a very a very deep and dangerous correspondence with the French Island of Mauritius.

1780, January. Some time in July, 1779, the majority in council resolved against the most pointed efforts to dissuade, on the parts of Mr. Francis and Mr. Wheler, to send another detachment, to consist of 2,500 effectives, under the command of Captain Popham, across the continent, to reinforce Colonel Goddard's army at Surat; and that the detachment be draughted from the Sepoy battalions up the country. The latter end of August, Captain Popham took leave, and received his last dispatches, particularly an order on the Resident at Oude for 278,832 current rupees, in part of the subsistence and contingencies of the expedition. The universal opinion throughout Hindostan prognosticated, that it was a direct sacrifice of so weak a body of troops, not having the most distant prospect of similar successful casualties, to favour their escape and passage, as the first detachment had, consisting of three times the number of experienced troops, connected battalions, and the compleatest train of artillery in Asia under the command of Major Bailie, who has long been considered as the ablest artillery officer in the service. It was confidently alledged, that the very officers, who are seldom backward to go upon enterprizing service, did not shew any eagerness to go upon this; and the desertion of many, and almost a total refusal of the rank and file, to cross the Jumna, yielded too convincing a proof of the sense the natives had entertained of the improbability of succeeding. This avowed disaffection prevented the march of the detachment, until a laughable, preposterous treaty with the poor reduced Rana, of the hilly country of Gohud, was solemnized in January or February, 1780, and the impractibility of the expedition being then acknowledged; to save appearances, Captain Popham's detachment were ordered to join the visionary veterans

of

of our great and powerful new ally, to reduce the fortress of Gucaliar, belonging to the Marrattas, in the neighbourhood of Gohud. The history of this famous treaty, and the embassy of state sent to witness the execution of a paper, having had already all the solemnity and authenticity usual and essential in India, is of a piece with many others, and worthy of perusal. *

It is a moral truth, that success against the Marratta Chief, Futta Sing Guiacawar, the Jaghire-dar of Guzzerat, does not immediately affect or injure the Regency of Poonah; nor will it ever be in the power of Colonel Goddard to attack them in their own country, or to bring them to a pitch or decisive battle in the field. They will pay no regard to any treaty or capitulation with Futta Sing, who, as a tenant for life, or in actual possession to his own sole use, has no right of alienation. They have always shewn an aversion to the payment of money by treaty, as much as they have plainly discovered a solicitous inclination to preserve an uninterrupted harmony and alliance with the English. The trade of Guzzerat is of more importance to the English trade to Bengal and China, than any revenue that can arise from the territorial possession thereof, under an English system of government. It would therefore have been more advantageous to the East India Company, and the British nation, to have submitted to a second total defeat, as the means of any tolerable accommodation, than to continue a war, the expence of which is altogether insupportable by the Company's funds, and which can have no other tendency than to exasperate the Marrattas, and to excite additional jealousy, dread, and combinations in all the other native powers. If the

war

---

* The minutes are published in a late pamphlet, containing abstracts of minutes on Contracts, &c. in 1779.

war has held out to the year 1781, it muſt inevitably have coſt the Company above three millions of pounds ſterling.

The fidelity of the Company's native troops hath been preſerved, and their military ſucceſſes have ariſen ſolely from a punctuality which no other power in India was able to obſerve in the payment of military eſtabliſhments, and from the regular diſcipline which, in conſequence of that punctuality, Britiſh officers were enabled to maintain in the armies. If the Company are rendered incapable of purſuing the ſame line of exactitude, mutiny and deſertion however dangerous, will have leſs fatal conſequences, than the occaſion which it will furniſh to their avowed enemies, of augmenting their armies with veteran troops, regularly formed and diſciplined by the Company themſelves. Such a ſpirit diſcovered itſelf in 1779, upon ſeveral occaſions, even in the brigade ſtationed in and near Fort William, and it became remarkably ſerious in General Goddard's army at Baroach. The Company's allies (if that appellation can be ſaid to belong to the ſtate of dependence in which they are held) are reduced to a ſtate of miſery and diſtreſs, and by mere oppreſſion rendered not only diſaffected, but both unable and unwilling to pay their ſubſidiary engagements. The Company's own provinces are depopulated, the Zemindars utterly unable to diſcharge the heavy load of arrears which is ſuſpended over them; their treaſures at each Preſidency are empty; their credit, faith, and power, are equally ſuſpected; their inveſtments, by ſolemn reſolutions, as an act of neceſſity, not of choice, reduced 40 per cent. in Bengal; the quality of the remaining inveſtment ſo debaſed, and its coſt ſo advanced, that the ſales in Europe create a certain large deficiency; their military and civil eſtabliſhments, in the very midſt of theſe dreadful ſymptoms, have been impolitically and madly augmented,

without

without bounds or measure; the estimate of probable resources for the year 1780 hath been acknowleged to fall grievously short of their absolute engagements;* and they are involved in a general war with all the independent states of Hindostan, and in the disaffection of their dependent allies, who are all encouraged and excited, by assurances of support from the only European powers who are conditioned to do it with effect. It is much to be dreaded, that the fatal blow is already struck, which may have blasted the glorious prospect of a vast accession of territory and trade in the British empire.

* Near 300,000 l. sterling, after consuming the deposit of 359,600 l. sterling, to answer the calls of any emergency.

London, 15th March, 1781.

POSTSCRIPT.

THE ungenerous and uncandid attempt by the partizans of the Governor General, to saddle the late incurſions of Hyder-Alli-Cawn into the Carnatic, and the diſaſter to the Madras army, on the Preſidency of Fort St. George, in order to draw the reproach which juſtly belong to them, from the meaſures of the Governor General, and the iniquitous Marratta war, into which he deliberately forced the Company, may bring forth ſome more documents, to place the ſaddle upon the right horſe. In the mean time, it is thought proper to ſubjoin to this narrative, an extract from a minute which Mr. Whitehill, the late Preſident of Fort St. George, committed upon record in Council, before he was ſuſpended by the Governor General and Council in November 1780, to ſhew that the Marratta war *alone*, excited Hyder-Alli-Cawn to commence hoſtilities againſt the Company, in confederacy with the Marrattas, and the reſt of the native powers, and even in alliance with Scha-Allum, and his Vizier Nudjiff-Cawn, whoſe abilities as a General and Politician, are diſtinguiſhed in Hindoſtan. In ſpeaking of the Governor General and Council, Mr. Whitehill uſes the following convictive language, every word of which being founded on facts, corroborate the predictions and cenſures conveyed in the preceding narrative.

" Plunged into almoſt inextricable difficulties, it is
" not an unwiſe ſtretch of policy, to ſcreen themſelves
" if

" if in their power; and to load others with the op-
" probium of those acts, which are now overpowering
" *us*, with the pernicious consequence of their effects."

" Possessed of a sufficiency of territory, more even
" than we were adequate to the management of, your
" Presidency of Bengal might surely have been content
" with paying a strict obedience to your orders, which
" have been uniform and strict on that head; but unfor-
" tunately for your affairs, the offensive line of conduct
" which they adopted against the Marrattas, threw them
" into a scene of action so extensive, and so full of diffi-
" culty, that neither their forces, nor their revenues,
" were capable of bearing them through with any pos-
" sibility of success. Had the experience of former
" times been called in a little to their aid, they would
" have seen that Aurengzebe, one of the most formid-
" able monarchs that ever sat upon the throne of Delhi,
" was, after a twenty years struggle with all the power
" and riches of Hindostan, obliged to abandon a similar
" attempt."

" It was not, however, in the line alone of hostility,
" that the Governor General and Council of Bengal,
" lost sight of the national interests which have been
" entrusted to their care."

" They unaccountably forgot them in their negoci-
" ations and alliances with the Marratta Chiefs. The
" infant Paishwa was first to be protected; next, Ro-
" ganaut-row was to be assisted; again, Moodajee Boo-
" sla was to be supported in some distant pretensions;
" and all to the same object, the supreme government
" of the Marratta state."

" When a contradiction of this nature appears in the
" public acts of a great power; when a more than a
" suspicion of the professions it may make, becomes
" the ruling complexion of the minds of those it is en-
" gaged with, the surest prop of political security is
" shaken, and every evil may be justly expected as the
" consequence."

"The measures that have been pursued in the pro-
"secution of this fatal Marratta contest, may indeed
"be supposed to be unconnected with the principle of
"this address; but the truth is, the Marratta war has
"been the real source of all the mischief that hath be-
"fallen the Carnatic, and of all the injury that hath
"been levelled at me by the Governor General and
"Council of Bengal. Had peace existed in that quar-
"ter with the English, Hyder-Alli-Cawn would never
"have ventured from his own dominions. He saw,
"however, the extremity to which we were reduced,
"(a considerable part of our troops having been de-
"tached to Bombay, at the requisition of the govern-
"ment of Bengal, for the support of this very war)
"and very prudently seized hold of the occasion to dis-
"tress us, where he knew we were most vulnerable."

"The Governor General and Council of Bengal,
"may, in exculpation of themselves, endeavour to
"brand this Presidency with the guilt of having ex-
"cited the troubles which at present exist in the Car-
"natic, by protracting the restitution of the Guntoor
"Circar, and of having driven the Nabob Nizam-
"Alli-Cawn, to avow himself the adviser of the con-
"federacy. But the original cause of almost the loss
"of all our consequence in Hindostan, will be found
"to arise from the rash and ruinous conduct that they
"themselves have held with respect to the Marrattas.
"In the South, it has enabled Hyder to carry fire and
"desolation before him; and in the North, (as the
"latest accounts inform us) it hath afforded a favour-
"able opportunity to the Mogul and Nudjiff-Cawn,
"to take the field with a considerable army, decla-
"redly with the intent of wresting from the English
"the country which they took from the Rohillas, and
"the dominions of Assoph-ul-Dowla, the Nabob of
"Oude."

APPENDIX.

APPENDIX.

A. No. I.

Copy of a Letter from Governor HASTINGS to DEWAGUR PUNDIT, Prime Minister to the Rajah of Berar, dated in Calcutta, 23d November, 1778.

"In the whole of my conduct I have departed from the common line of policy, and have made advances, when others, in my situation, would have waited for solicitations; as the greatest advantages to which I can look, cannot in their nature equal those to which the prosperous issue of our measures, may conduct the state of the Maha Rajah's government. But I know the characters to which I address myself. I trust to the approved bravery and spirit of your Chief, that he will ardently catch at the objects presented to his ambition, and to your wisdom; of which, if fame reports truly, no minister ever possessed a larger portion, that you will view their importance in too clear a light to hazard the loss of them, by attempting to take an advantage of the desire which I have expressed for their accomplishment. This intimation is not so much intended for a caution to you, as for an explanation of my conduct to those who may be less able to penetrate into the grounds of it."

A. No. II.

Copy of a letter from MOODAGEE BOOSLA to Governor HASTINGS, dated the 5th December, 1778, and received the 2d January, 1779.

"Your friendly letter of the 19th Ramzam, (11th October) informing me of your having received advice of the death of Mr. Elliot, in his way to Naigpore; your concern at that event, and at the unavoid-

a   able

able suspensions of the negotiations which that gentleman was to have conducted with me on the part of your government, and the delay in the establishment of a strict and perpetual friendship between the Companys' state and mine (concerning which you had exerted yourself so warmly) by reason that the present situation of affairs would not admit of the delay which must attend the deputation of another person from thence without injuring the designs in hand; but that in your conviction of my favorable disposition, from the knowledge that my interests and the Companys' are inseparably connected, and in the zeal of Beneram Pundit, whom, during the long period he resided with you, you found so deserving of your confidence, &c. &c. &c. *That in the plan proposed*, and what you have written, is to promote our common advantage, not for the interest of one party only, being convinced that no public alliance or *private friendship*, can be firmly established without *reciprocal* advantages. That it is on these principles *you had long ago planned an alliance with me*; the time for the accomplishment of which is *now come*: for you conceive it to be equally for my interest as for yours; our countries bordering on each other, and our natural enemies being the same. That in a word, you required nothing but the junction of my forces with yours, by which, though each is singly very powerful, they will acquire a ten-fold proportion of strength. *That the delay of the progress in the detachment intended for Bombay, had not arisen from the opposition of an enemy, but from other causes improper to mention; but that it will now shortly arrive in my territories, and its operation be determined by my advice. That you have given directions to Colonel Leslie, to co-operate with the forces which I shall unite with his*: That as you offer me the forces of your Circar to promote my views, you in return require the assistance of mine to effect your purposes;

poses; with other particulars which I fully understand, reached me on the 26th Shawand (16th November) afforded me great pleasure.——I also received duplicate and triplicate of this letter; in the latter part of it you express, that as you have made me acquainted with your views, it is necessary that I also communicate to you, without reserve, the ends which I look to for my advantage in this union.——That the good faith of the English to every engagement they contract, so long as it is observed by others, is universally known; and that it has been the invariable rule of your conduct, to support this character in all acts depending on you, and never to relinquish any design of importance formed on good and judicious grounds; but to persevere steadily to its completion. *That having thus explained to me your sentiments and views, you wait only to know mine; and on the knowledge of these you shall form your ultimate resolution.*

It is equally a maxim of sincere friendship and good government, steadiness, magnanimity, and foresight, that a plan formed on good and judicious grounds, should be conducted in such a manner, as to end happily: *You desire to learn my sentiments and views, and deferring to form your ultimate resolutions, 'till you had heard further from me, is the same thing, as if you had consulted me primarily on your first designs.*

Since, after the strictest scrutiny and researches into the dispositions and views of the multitude, it has been determined on proofs of mutual sincerity and good faith, that a perpetual friendship and union be established, it will, like the wall of Alexander, for the happiness of mankind, continue unshaken until the end of time.

a 2 The

The having caused a translation to be made into English of the Hindoo books, called the Shaster and Poran, and of the history of the former Kings, the studying these books, and keeping the pictures of the former Kings and present rulers of Hind, Decan, &c. always before your eyes, and from their lifeless similitude to discover which of them were, or are worthy of rule, and possessed of good faith, from which to determine with whom to contract engagements, and what conduct to observe to them respectively.——Also the endeavour to preserve the blessing of peace, 'till forced to relinquish it.——The supporting every one in his hereditary right,—and revenging the breach of faith and engagements: but on the submission of the offenders, the exercise of the virtues of clemency and generosity by pardoning, and receiving him again into favor, and restoring him to his possessions—*the not suffering the intoxication of power to reduce you into a breach of faith, and the giving support to each illustrious house in proportion to its respective merits*;——And in matters which required a long course of years to bring to perfection, the forming your conduct on mature deliberation, and the advice of the Company and Council, are the sure means of exalting your greatness and prosperity to the highest pitch.——The intention of all this is to recommend universal peace and friendship in the manner following. The almighty disposes of kingdoms, and places whomsoever he chuses on the seats of power and rule; but makes their stability to depend on their peaceable, just, and friendly conduct to others.— It is not every one who is equal to the task of government, on the plan designed by the almighty ruler, and of ensuring his stability, by a wise and just conduct.— Hind and Decan possess, at present, very few enlightened, but a great multitude of weak and ignorant men. The English Chiefs, and you in a superior degree, possess

sess all the virtues above recited, who coming from distant islands by a six month's voyage on the great ocean, by their magnanimity and fortitude, gained the admiration of many Soubahs on this continent. It is easy to acquire a kingdom; but to become a King over Kings, and Chief of Chiefs, is a very difficult matter. ——The attainment of this is only to be effected by the means of friendship, by which the universe may be subjected. My conduct is framed on these principles. —— The residence of Beneram Pundit at Calcutta, was solely to effect the establishment of the most intimate friendship, and by the blessing of God it has taken such deep root that, through your means, it has reached the ears of the Company and King of England; and our connection and correspondence carried on under the veil of the vicinity of our dominions, has been discovered by the Poonah Ministers, and by the Nabob Nizum-ul-Dowla; yet, though they form various conjectures and doubts, and have sent a trusty Vakeel, and written repeated letters, to endeavour to find out the motives of our union, yet they remain a mystery; as I make the plea of our ancient ties, and the junction of our territories.

I was impatiently expecting the arrival of Mr. Elliot, who being endowed with an enlightened understanding, and invested with full powers from you to conduct the negotiations, and determine on the measures to be pursued, would have established the ties of a perpetual friendship, and have settled every matter on the firmest basis. It pleased God that he should die on the journey, and the grief I felt at his unfortunate loss, who would have been the means of settling all points between us, to our mutual content, and by his negociation with me, giving satisfaction to the Paishwa and Nabob Nizam ul-Dowla; all which have been by his death thrown back many months; my grief is not to be described, and only serves to add to your affliction. I have not yet recovered the shock which the event gave me, as you will learn more fully from Beneram Pundit. There is no remedy for such misfortunes, and it is in vain to strive against the decrees of providence; had Mr. Elliot arrived, *such strokes of policy would have been employed, that the Poonah Ministers would have adhered more scrupulously than before to their engagements; and the French, who are the natural enemies of the English, would have been theirs likewise; and their suspicions from apprehensions of support being given to Ragunaut-Row, which never was, nor is designed by the English Chiefs, as I learn from Beneram, who had it from your own mouth, and which has caused them great uneasiness, would have been entirely removed by Mr. Elliot and my joint security.*

The Nabob Nizam-ul-Dowla, who wrote you repeatedly on this subject, and received for answer, that you had no idea of aiding or supporting Ragunaut-Row, that your enmity was solely pointed against the French, and that whoever assisted the French were your enemies, would likewise by these means have been thoroughly satisfied, and your detachment would have reached Bombay, without meeting the smallest interruption; and had the Poonah Ministers then acted a contrary part, I should have withdrawn myself from their friendship. But by the death of Mr. Elliot, all these designs have fallen to the ground, and must be suspended 'till another opportunity, and the knowledge of your sentiments. *It is a proverb, that whatever is deliberately done, is well done.* In reply to what you write respecting your framing your ultimate resolutions, I have communicated to Beneram Pundit whatever I judge proper and eligible, and which may promote them in such a manner as may not be subject to any change from the

vicissi-

vicissitudes of fortune; for those points which I fixed on, after minute deliberation, as the most eligible that can be adopted, I refer you to the letters of Beneram Pundit. If, notwithstanding, you have any plan to propose for the reciprocal benefit of our states, be pleased to communicate to me.

Postscript.

To your letter, respecting sending an army to overawe the French, and to reinforce the Government of Bombay, and setting forth that the Poona Ministers having broken the treaty with the English, and in opposition to the rights of friendship received an Envoy of the French King, and granted the port of Choul to that nation, thereby enabling them to form an arsenal, and collect military stores, and of their having written to their officers, to permit the French ships to enter their ports, and that it being therefore incumbent on you to take measures to counteract their designs, you had determined to send a strong detachment for the reinforcement of Bombay, by the route of Berar; and that in consideration of our ancient friendship, and the vicinity of our dominions, you requested that on its arrival in my neighbourhood, I would cause it to be instructed in the route, and providing it with provisions and necessaries, have it conducted in safety through my territories, and join a body of my forces with it, which would increase and cement our friendship; and that you have, at the assurance of Beneram, fixed on this route for its march in preference to any other.——
In reply to this letter, actuated by its dictates of the sincerest friendship, I waited not to take the advice of any one, but without hesitation wrote you.——That where a sincere friendship existed, the passage of troops through my country was a matter of no moment.

that

that they should proceed immediately through my country.——I likewise informed Colonel Leslie of the difficulties and dangers he would meet with in the way, from dangerous mountains, extensive rivers, &c. And also dispatched Lalla Jadda Roy, with a Chief of note, to the banks of the Narbudda, to supply the detachment with provisions, as long as they were in my territory, and to treat them with all the duties of hospitality; where he waited in expectation of their arrival for six months to no purpose. *They loitered away their time in the Bundle Cund countries, contrary to every rule of policy.*——At that time all the Poonah Ministers were separately employed in their own private affairs, or in the war with Hyder Naig, insomuch that they had no time to turn their attention to the concerns of other parts, and the march to Bombay might have been effected with the greatest ease. The time is now past. The arrow is shot, and cannot be recalled. As I have repeatedly written to the Poonah Ministers, with whom I keep up a correspondence on the subject of their encouraging a French Envoy, and breaking their faith with the English Chiefs, acts highly inconsistent with honour and policy. The answer I have received from them, I have communicated to you. The substance of what they say in their own justification is this. That the French Vakeel came for the purpose of traffic; not to negociate; yet, for the satisfaction of the English, they gave him his dismission. That the account of the grant of the port of Choul, and an arsenal, is entirely without foundation; and that they have not the least indisposition towards the English; that I will therefore write to Calcutta, that you may be perfectly satisfied respecting their disposition. My letters did not produce the effect of satisfying you on the subject of the Paishwa, but your doubts still remained. And, actuated by

wisdom

wisdom and prudence, you determined to send Mr. Elliot to me, and wrote to me, that on his arrival at Naigpore, after he had an interview with me, and learned my sentiments and views, he would, in conjunction with me, form a plan for our mutual honour and benefit, and give directions to Cononel Leslie in consequence, who would be guided thereby.——The event of this gentleman's deputation is too well known, and Cononel Leslie likewise, after engaging in hostilities with the Paishwa's officers, and Zimendars of these parts, and collecting large sums of money, died. Colonel Goddard succeeded to the command, and pursued the same line of conduct, with respect to the Talookdars as his predecessor. And arriving at Garawale and Garasur in the territory of the Afghans, whither he was obliged to march with the utmost caution, being surrounded with a Marratta army, who constantly seized every opportunity to attack him, wrote me from thence, that he should shortly reach the Narbudda, where I would be pleased to cause grain and other necessaries to be prepared, and a party of my forces to be ready to join him.——I wrote him in answer, that Lalla Jada Roy, and Shao Baal Hazaile were waiting on that side the Narbudda, which is within my territories, and that the gaut where the troops should cross was two cofs from hence under Haffingabad; that Janojee Boosla forded it with his army at that place, on his expedition to Malawa, and that I did not doubt it was now fordable; that he should therefore cross his army there, and repair to Haffingabad; that Lalla Jada Roy would exert his utmost assiduity in supplying him with grain and other provisions, and treat them with every degree of hospitality; but that, as the road forward was very difficult and dangerous, and thousands of the Balha Castes, were concealed in the holes in the mountains; who though not able to oppose him openly, yet would do it by ambufcade and ftratagems, and cut off his fupplies of provifions: and that, beyond that he would enter the Soubafhip of Barhampore, dependant on the Paifhwa; that near 4000 of Scindia's cavalry were waiting at the fort of Affur, for the arrival of the Englifh on the banks of the Ganges; 10,000 more were under the command of Bagarut Sundiab; Scindiah himfelf with the chiefs in readinefs at Poona, waiting to hear of the approach of the Englifh. And moreover in Berar, in which the Nabob Nizam-ul-Dowla, poffeffes a fhare with me; all the Jaghirdars were in readinefs with powerful armies; and although the Englifh poffeffed the greateft magnanimity in battle, yet as every ftep they took would be juft into the mouth of danger, and all the above-mentioned chiefs would fet themfelves to cut off and deftroy his provifions, and take every opportunity of attacking him when they faw an advantage, and of harraffing him night and day; conftantly furrounding his army with their numerous forces, the junction of a body of my forces with his, would avail nothing in the face of fuch large armies; but would only involve me in the greateft loffes. That it neither was advifeable for him to return, which would diminifh the awe and refpect in which he was held: That I would therefore write the particulars explicitly to Calcutta, and that whatever you fhould think proper to intimate to him and me in reply, it would be advifeable to abide by, and act accordingly. All which time, I would recommend that he continued at Hoffingur——That I have received letters from Calcutta, filled with the warmeft friendfhip and confidence to the following purport; " That the detachment fhould come into my neighbourhood, and be guided in its operations by my advice:" that it is incumbent on every Chief who enjoys the confidence of another, to give fuch advice as may

be

be most advantageous to the party reposing trust, and most consistent with the faith of engagaments; and that with such conduct the Almighty is well pleased. That I had also written to the Poonah Ministers my advice on the situation of affairs to this purport.
" That Mr. Elliot was deputed hither to negociate
" with me; but dying in the journey, all the nego-
" ciations intrusted to him were suspended: that had he
" arrived at Naigpore, I had determined, from princi-
" ples of attachment, to have removed from the
" minds of the English the doubts and apprehensions
" which had arrisen, by reason of the supposed, en-
" couragement of the French Envoy at Poonah, and
" the agreement to support that nation, who were
" the inveterate enemies of the English, which had
" given rise to the quarrel between the two states, by
" proving to them under the sanction of solemn oaths,
" and becoming myself guarrantee, that all those
" reports were groundless, and that the Poonah Mi-
" nisters were steady and zealous in their engagements
" with the English; and on several accounts highly
" obliged to them: and I would have taken, from
" Mr. Elliot, engagements that the English had no
" idea of affording support to Raganaut-Row, but
" were resolved to maintain their treaty inviolate;
" and that their apprehensions related to the French,
" and that when I gave the English satisfaction, rela-
" ting to the French, and become guarantee, all his
" doubts would be removed; and that if it was re-
" quisite a fresh engagement should be executed, to
" which he would be a guarantee; that in brief each
" party entertained a reasonable doubt; the English,
" that the Poonah Ministers would join with the
" French; and the Poonah Ministers, that the English
" support Roganaut-Row; that when these suspicions
" no longer remained, all causes of displeasure would
" of course cease, and that they could have no objection

" to a detachment of English forces sent for the rein-
" forcement of Bombay, and to overawe the French,
" not for the support of Roganaut-Row, repairing
" thither, and to oppose them, would in such case
" have been highly improper." &c. &c. &c.

Second Postscript.

Baboo-Row, the Paishaw's Vakeel, has observed to me in the course of conversation, that his master has not the slightest idea of failing in his engagements with the English, or of contracting any friendship with the French, but that the treaty forbids the march of English forces through the Paishwa's dominions; that therefore the appearance of the detachment now on its march, is an infringement of the treaty.

Third Postscript.

Although it may appear improper to repeat the same thing over again, yet the importance of the subject may plead in my excuse. On either part a doubt subsists. The Poonah Ministers suspect that the English forces on their march to Bombay, though ostensibly for the purpose of opposing the French, are in reality intended for the support of Roganaut-Row; and that the English at Bombay, who were not included in the treaty with the Paishwa, which was concluded through the Government of Bengal, with the advice of the Chief at Calcutta, are desirous of breaking with the Paishwa, and supporting Roganaut-Row, and that the detachment had been sent at their requisition. They alledge, that the Chief of Calcutta, writes to them, that he is firmly resolved to adhere to the treaty with the Paishwa, and that the detachment he has sent to Bombay is solely to awe the French, without the

least

least design to assist Roganaut-Row; and that since it is forbidden in the treaty to dispatch troops over land, the march of the troops is a breach of it. That if it is necessary to send troops to Bombay, to awe the French, they ought to be sent by sea.

The English on their part suspect the Poonah Ministers of joining the French, in consequence of having received a French Vakeel. As the Paishwa formerly wrote me, that he had no idea of failing in his engagements with the English, and that he had given no encouragement to the French Vakeel, who came for the purpose of traffic, and that he had dismissed him, therefore requested that I would satisfy you in that respect. I, in consequence, formerly wrote you all these particulars. As I have a voucher in my hand from the Paishwa, that he has no connection with the French, and is steady to his engagements with the English, I am able, by this voucher, to give you complete satisfaction on this head. But I have no voucher, or intimation from you, by which I may be able to give satisfaction to him.

As he pleads a prohibition in the treaty, to the march of forces over land, and likewise complains respecting the money collected by Colonel Leslie in his territories. What answer can be made thereto?

As the time requires, that a reconciliation take place with the Poonah Ministers, you will consider and determine what reply shall be given to these two points of which they complain, and by what means they may be satisfied, and communicate your resolution to me, that I may write conformable thereto, and remove all doubts.

A. No.

A. No. III.

Mr. Francis's *minute on the letter from* Moodajee Boosla, *dated* 5th December, 1778.

January 11, 1779.

I have nothing to object to the pious precepts, and excellent moral instructions contained in these letters. Whether they come seasonably or not, at a time when deep plans of policy, and decided acts of vigour might have been expected from our intended ally, instead of a general discourse upon the duties of a statesman. Or how far such a discourse may with propriety be addressed to the chief member of this government, are questions very little necessary to be considered at present. It is of no sort of moment to us now, to enquire into the moral character, or religious creed of this Marratta, though it might have been prudent in us to have been somewhat better acquainted with both, before we trusted him so far. From other parts of his letter we may collect information of a more interesting nature. If we really mean the public service, if we mean to save Colonel Goddard's army, and to provide for the security of the Company's possessions, let us not obstinately shut our eyes to the evidence before us. After examining the facts without prejudice or passion, let us draw the natural and obvious conclusions from these facts, and endeavour to act firmly and consistently upon both.

For my own part, the declarations contained in Moodajee Boosla's letter to Colonel Goddard, received on the 21st of December, appeared to me sufficiently explicit. A majority of the Board, however, still thought it necessary to wait for some further explanation.
But

But now I presume that not the shadow of a doubt can remain with any of us concerning his real sentiments and resolutions. The most material points of fact ascertained by the present letters, and by which our measures must be immediately directed, are

1st. That so late as the 5th of December, Moodajee Boosla does not appear to have had the least idea of the extent or nature of the Governor-General's views, in the proposed alliance, though we have been informed that his Vakeel, Beneram Pundid, was perfectly possessed of the project of that alliance, from several conversations which he has had with the Governor-General in Calcutta, and was authorized to commmnicate the same to his master.

2dly. That whatever degree of information the Rajah might possess on this subject, and admitting his ignorance of the Governor's plan to be merely affected, he appears plainly to have had no sort of disposition *to catch at the objects presented to his ambition,* or to run the risque of a rupture either with the Paishwa or the Nizam, much less with both at the same instant, for any offers that we can make him. On this point his declarations are clear and decided.

3dly. That so far from shewing a disposition to join us against his countrymen, he says expressly, " that " the junction of a body of his forces with Colonel " Goddard's would avail nothing in the face of such " large armies, but would only involve himself in the " greatest losses."

4thly. That it is his opinion, founded on reason, which, if he does not deceive us, are sufficiently solid, that the detachment cannot proceed towards Bombay,

without

without the greatest difficulty and danger, nor return without disgrace.

5thly,—That so far from entering into an offensive alliance with us against the Poona government, he insists on the necessity of our coming to an immediate conciliation with them, and of our previously giving them satisfaction for the march of our army through their country, and for the large sums collected from their dominions, first by Colonel Leslie, and afterwards by Colonel Goddard, " who (he says) has pur- " sued the same line of conduct, with respect to the " Talookdars, as his predecessors."——The perusal of these voluminous letters, will suggest many other interesting reflections to our superiors. One circumstance in particular, I think deserves their notice, notwithstanding the detachment was for some months under the orders of the Presidency of Bombay, whose designs were very explicitly communicated to us, and although the commanding officer was intreated to co-operate with them in the plan they had formed for the support of Ragoba, and notwithstanding all the measures taken here, professedly originated from the communications which were received in January last, of certain overtures supposed to have been made by the Ministers for reinstating Ragoba. Moodajee Boosla now affirms, that his Vakeel *had it from Mr. Hastings's own mouth, that it never was, nor is designed by the English Chiefs to support Ragoba.*

The good advice contained in these letters is, in effect, the severest reflections on the levity and precipitancy of our councils; and probably has no other meaning, than to shew the Governor General in what respect Moodajee Boosla holds a statesman, who professes " to have departed from the common line of po-
" licy

"licy in the whole of his conduct."—If we were not become the objects of his scorn, would our boasted ally take such a time as this to tell us, " that it is a pro-
" verb, that whatever is deliberately done is well done ;
" that it will be proper maturely to *deliberate* on the
" probable event before the commencement of any un-
" dertaking, and that it is the part of wisdom and sound
" judgment, before any further steps are taken, to de-
" termine by what means they are to be supported,
" that no unsteadiness may hereafter arise."

What must this Marratta think of the prudence of a government that sends an army a thousand miles forward into an enemy's country, in the presumption of receiving assistance on the spot, without any treaty previously concluded; without a single condition agreed on; without one stipulation formed for the operations, for the proceeding, or for the retreat of that army; and even without knowing the general sentiments, views, or dispositions of the prince on whose future support we placed our dependance? I do not wonder that Moodajee Boosla should feel no inclination to unite his fortune with such a government.—But let us now at least profit by his advice, as far as the circumstances we are reduced to will admit. In the natural order of things, deliberation should go before measures, with us it must follow them.

Colonel Goddard's army is now near eleven degrees west of Calcutta. We have no other way of tracing his progress, or ascertaining his distance from us, but by observing, as accurately as we can, the latitude and longitude of his position, on a general map of India. If he attempts to proceed, it must be *in the mouth of danger*. If he retreats, *it will reflect dishonour on our arms*. If he advances into Berar, it is against the advice

c of

of the Rajah, who infifts on his remaining where he is; and who, I prefume, will never fuffer an Englifh army to march into the heart of the country; efpecially when he hears that another detachment is preparing to enter it from the eaftward. This meafure, fo far from giving him encouragement to join us, muft naturally fill him with jealoufy and diftruft. Without infifting on the faithlefs character uniformly attributed to the Marrattas, thefe motives alone are fufficient to put him on his guard againft us; while others, equally powerful, may induce him to take advantage of the critical fituation of our army, and to compromife his own differences with the Paifhwa and the Nizam at our expence. At all events, I prefume, it cannot be difputed, that the fafety of the detachment depends greatly on the good faith of Moodajee Boofla. In this fituation we have a choice of difficulties before us; whatever refolution we adopt will, I fear, be liable to fuch objections as will admit of no better anfwer, than that ftill greater objections may be urged againft any other. We may order Colonel Goddard, at all events, to proceed to Bombay; or to move towards our weftern frontiers through Berar, or to return as expeditioufly as he can, by the way he went. I am againft the firft, becaufe I am convinced it cannot be attempted without the greateft hazard to the detachment, or with the fmalleft probability of fuccefs. I confider it as one common and equally effential intereft of all the powers of India to oppofe the march of an Englifh army acrofs the continent; and, by defeating the attempt in the firft inftance, to deter us from ever forming fuch a enterprize again. Moodajee Boofla himfelf ftates the danger to us in terms which fufficiently exprefs his opinion of the impoffibility of furmounting it.

With

With respect to Bombay, notwithstanding all that has been said of the deep designs of the French, that place is actually in no danger; if it were, this is not the way of providing for its defence. I am against the second, because it appears that the Rajah himself is very averse to letting Colonel Goddard come into his country, and insists on his staying where he is. If the army should move into Berar without his consent, and without some stipulations previously determined with him, it will be always in his power to sacrifice them to the Poonah Government, or to the Nizam, if they can make it their interest so to do. For my own part, I am very much inclined to think, that all his late delays and uncertainties are affected, for no other purpose but to give his countrymen time to complete their preparations, and to surround Colonel Goddard. No choice then is left, but to order Colonel Goddard to return as he went. I do not say, that this measure shall not lessen the opinion which the powers of India may hitherto have entertained of the councils of this government. It may also be thought in some degree disgraceful to our arms. But neither is this of weight against other superior considerations; nor do I apprehend that if no direct impression be made upon our army, its bare retreat will prove any thing, but the extreme imprudence of those measures which have left us no other option. At the same time, I think that proper letters should be written to the Paishwa, to inform him of this alteration, to desire that the army may return without molestation, and to assure him that we are sincerely disposed to come to a conciliation with him, and to adjust whatever differences may unfortunately have arisen between his government and ours, in an amicable manner, agreeable to the terms and principles of the treaty of Poonah.

The time which has elapsed since the receipt of Moodajee Boosla's letters, and the critical situation of the detachment, make it indispensibly necessary that some clear and decisive orders be immediately dispatched to Colonel Goddard. I shall be ready to correct and alter my opinion, if I see just and solid reasons urged against it.

P. Francis.

Governor General. I have seen Mr. Francis's minute, *and do not think it necessary or proper to apply to it.*

W. Hastings.

Intelligence from Poona, *contained in a Letter from* Row Gee, *dated* 18*th of* January, 1779, *to the Nabob of* Arcot.

1. I have addressed your Highness several letters of late, some of which I hope are arrived. I have accounts of others having been intercepted in the road, and shall therefore recapitulate some of the most important transactions here.

2. The English Surdars, as I have already wrote to your Highness, marched from Bombay to the passes, and fortified that of Kodtichully. Raganaut-Row took possession of two forts which were in the road, and joined the English army, which I hear consisted of 700 Europeans, 8 batalions of Seapoys, 40 pieces of cannon, mortars, and a quantity of powder and military stores; they had besides 4 lacks of rupees in money.

3. Siccaram Pundit, and Nana Furnese, two Maratta Surdars, joined their forces, and satisfied the discontented

contented chiefs Schindiah and Holkar, by giving them money, jaghires, and other presents.

4. All the chiefs having met to consult what was to be done in the present state of affairs, they all with one voice agreed, that if Roganaut-Row came with his own forces alone, they should receive him, and give him a share of the power as formerly; but since he came with an army of English, who were of a different nation from them, and whose conduct in Sujah Dowla's country, the Rohilla country, Bengal, and the Carnatic, they were well acquainted with; they unanimously determined not to receive Roganaut-Row; as otherwise, in the end, they would be obliged to forsake their religion, and become the slaves of Europeans. Upon this they exchanged oaths; and Nehum-Row, Apagee Pundit, and Scindiah, were sent with an army of 15,000 horse, besides foot, to the Gaut of Telicanoon, and were followed immediately after by Siccaram Pundit and Nana Furneze, with 40,000 horse.

5. It has been for some time the fixed determination of the English Surdars to give their assistance to Roganaut-Row, in replacing him at the head of the government; an army was sent from Calcutta, who made an alliance with Boosla, (Rajah of Berar) and they were greatly encouraged by the news of the surrender of Pondicherry.

6. Mr. Mostyn, who went from Poonah, made them believe, that many of the Marratta Surdars were in their interest, and that as soon as their army should arrive at the Gaut, Holkar would join them with all his forces.

7. The

7. The English, trusting to this, marched their army to the Gaut, and waited impatiently for a whole month, but no one appeared to join their standard. The English army marched forward from the Gaut, and were so much harrassed by the Marattas as not to be able to proceed more than two cofs a day, during which time they lost a great many of their men by the fire kept upon them by the Marattas. When they came to Chockly, which is about 14 cofs from the pafs, they were obliged to halt; Captain Stewart, one of their Surdars, was killed at this place.

8. On the 21st January the European army arrived at Tulicanoon (17 cofs from the pafs) Mr. Carnac, Second of Bombay, was with them. Siccaram sent a body of horse to Tulicanoon, to harrafs them; 25 Europeans, amongst whom was an officer, and 100 fepoys, were killed on the first day; the Marattas had 200 men killed.

9. On the 2d day, the English were furrounded on all sides by the Marattas, and all supplies of provisions cut off from them. Seeing themselves in this situation, they determined, if poffible, to return back by the Gaut, and confulted upon the means to effect it. Roganaut-Row hearing this, sent privately to the Marattas Chief, Sindiah, telling him, that if he would attack the English, he would join them with his two battalions of Sepoys, and 600 horse. The English, it would appear, had intelligence of this; for, on the 13th January, they suddenly marched secretly from Tulicanoon, taking Roganaut-Row with them, and leaving their baggage and tents standing, under the protection of 200 Europeans, and one battalion of Sepoys, with eight pieces of cannon, to make the Marattas believe that their whole force was at Tulicanhoon.——Siccaram, however,

however, got private intelligence of their march; and he, with Nana Furneze, Scindiah, and Holkar, went to cut off their march. At the same he sent a body of horse to Tulicanoon, where the rest of the English were encamped. The Marattas, as usual, fell upon the plunder, and a smart engagement ensued between them and the English. The detachment, who had marched with Roganaut-Row, had not proceeded far, returned to the assistance of those in their camp. A heavy cannonade was kept up by the Marattas from midnight till four o'clock the next day; the English were not able to march one foot of way, and all their firing took no effect; 150 Europeans, with many of their officers, and 800 Sepoys were killed. The Marattas surrounded them, and kept patroles going all night, to prevent any from escaping. On the 14th, the Marattas commenced their cannonading again, 50 Europeans, and 400 Sepoys were killed. The English ceased firing, seeing that it had no effect. In the evening of that day, the servant of Roganaut-Row, and that of Mr. Carnac, brought a letter to Madah Row, acquainting him that they would send a trusty person to confer with him upon some matters, if leave was given. The Surdars read the letter, and sent an answer by the same person, that they were willing to cease hostilities, until a person was sent. They, however, took care to keep a strict patrole round the English camp all night. On the 15th the Marattas Surdars went to the trenches, and began firing again; but it was not answered from the English camp: soon after, Mr. Farmer (a gentleman who was some time ago at your Highness's court) came from the English camp, and the fire of the Marattas immediately ceased. The Marattas sent for him into the presence, and Mr. Farmer said to them, "We are only merchants.——When "disputes prevailed with you, Raganaut-Row came to "us

"us, and demanded our protection. We thought he
"had a right to the government, and gave him our
"affistance. Nothing but ill fortune attends him, and
"we have been brought to this miferable ftate, by
"keeping him with us. You are mafters to keep him
"from us. We fhall henceforth adhere to the treaties
"that have formerly taken place between us. Be
"pleafed to forgive what had happened."

The Minifter anfwered. "Raganaut-Row is one of
"us. What right could you have to interfere in our
"concerns with him; We now defire you to give up
"Salfette and Baffin, and what other countries you
"have poffeffed yourfelves of; as alfo the Circars, thofe
"of the Purgunnahs of Baroch, &c. which you have
"taken in Guzzart. Adhere to the treaty made in
"the time of Bajalee Row, and afk nothing elfe."——
Mr. Farmer heard this anfwer, and returned to his
camp. While this negociation was carrying on, 15,000
Maratta horfe were fent againft fome out-pofts where
the Englifh had entrenched themfelves, and fet fire to
them, putting every one they met with to death. They
did the fame at the fort of Choul, where the Englifh
had fortified. I heard all this from Nana Furnize;
whether it be true or falfe, I am not certain.

On the 6th at noon, Mr. Farmer returned, and told
Schindiah that he had brought a blank paper, figned
and fealed, which the Maratta Chiefs might fill up as
they pleafed. Schindiah told the Minifters, that although
they had it in their power to make any demands they
p'eafed, it would not be advifeable to do it at this time.
"For our making large demands, would only fow re-
"fentment in their hearts, and we had better demand
"only what is neceffary. Let Roganaut-Row be with
"us, and the treaty between us and the Englifh will
"be

"be adhered to. Let Salsette and the Purgunnah in Guzzarats, &c. be given back to us. Let the Bengal army return back. For the rest let us act with them, as it is stipulated in the treaty with Balagee Row; let the jewels mortgaged by Roganaut-Row be restored, and nothing demanded for them. Let all these articles be wrote out on the paper which they have sent." Which was accordingly done.

"It is likewise conditioned, that till this treaty is returned, signed and sealed by the Governor of the Council, and select Committee, under the Company's seal, and till Salsette and the other countries be given up, the nephew of Captain Stewart and Mr. Farmer shall remain in the Maratta camp as hostages for the due performance of the articles of this treaty. The English soldiers who have escaped with their lives, fasted for three days, and are now in a miserable condition. The Europeans and Sepoys have all grounded their arms.—On the 17th the treaty was sent to the Maratta camp. The articles were written in Persian, Maratta, and English, sealed with the Company's seal, and signed by Mr. Carnac and seven officers. After this the Maratta Surdars sent them victuals, which they needed much. The English marched out, *escorted by* 2000 *Maratta horse*; but Roganaut-Row, not finding a lucky hour, did not go to the Maratta camp, but will go after 12 o'clock to-morrow, &c."

A. No. V.

Copy of a Letter from SICCARAM PUNDIT, Prime-Minister of the Poonah Government, to Governor-General HASTINGS.—Received in Bengal the 7th of December, 1778.

At the time when some of the Company's Chiefs were engaged in disputes and hostilities with the Chiefs of this government, actuated by a wish to promote the good and happiness of mankind in general, which suffered by those troubles, you interposed your friendly mediation, to remove the causes of complaint, and to put a stop to them; and deputed Colonel Upton for this purpose, to the presence of my master Scriminust Row, Row Pundit Pinkham, Pishaw Saib.

At the time of the ratification of peace, I objected to there being no person of rank and credit present on the part of the governor of Bombay; to which the Colonel made answer, "That the Governor and Supreme Coun-
"cil of Calcutta were invested with authority over all
"settlements of the English Company, and that their
"acts were binding on the Chiefs of all the English set-
"tlements." On the faith of this declaration, I made peace between this Government and the Company's Chiefs, and concluded a treaty; but the Governor of Bombay, has in every instance of his conduct since, excited troubles and commotions, in violation of the ties of friendship; and notwithstanding your express orders to expel Roganaut-Row from the Company's dominions, and to settle all points between the two states, in conformity to the treaty, he has performed nothing thereof. And an envoy from the King of France arriving here with a letter, interested persons, and inventors

of

of falshoods, conceiving this a lucky opportunity to obtain credit to their lying reports, without examination or reflection, reprefented it in the manner beft calculated to anfwer their malicious purpofes.

I call God to witnefs, that out of regard to the friendship and alliance of the Company and the English chiefs, I difmiffed the faid Envoy, without negociating, or even converfing with him.——I have lately heard, that fome of your people have hoftilely poffeffed themfelves of the fort of Calpee, which belongs to this government. This meafure is widely removed from the faith of the folemn treaty executed by the Englifh.

When the governor of Bombay, in former times, put on the mafk of friendfhip for the purpofes of deceit, and aided the enemies of this government; regarding you, Sir, as fuperior to all other Chiefs, I made peace and friendfhip with you; and thefe are the fruits produced by this friendfhip.

You write that the maintaining of friendfhip and ftrict union between our refpective ftates, is your refolve. Is it in effect for the prefervation of friendfhip that you trouble the dominions of this government? Such a mode of conduct is inconfiftent with the maxims and meafures of high and illuftrious Chiefs.—— It is mutually incumbent on us to preferve inviolate the terms of the treaty. Should any deviation arife therein, they are effects of the will and difpenfation of God.

A. No. VI.

From the same.———Received in Calcutta, the 12th December, 1778.

"I have been favoured with your letter under date the 22d Trēmadee Aſſamee (17th July) on the ſubject of the preſervation and increaſe of the friendſhip between the two ſtates, and intimating that it is your firſt reſolve to maintain every article of the treaty, ſo long as it is adhered to by the Paiſhwa; that the troops have been ſent ſolely for the reinforcement of the ſettlement of Bombay; and that the commanding officer had ſtrict injunctions to obſerve ſuch a conduct in every reſpect, as is conſiſtent with the friendſhip ſubſiſting; that the ſeveral letters you have lately received from this quarter, meaning from me, contain a declaration to maintain the treaty of friendſhip between us; yet that my having hitherto evaded to grant paſſes for the march of the troops through the government dominions, cauſes you great aſtoniſhment. That if I ſtill refuſe to comply therewith, you are remedileſs, and the blame will fall on me. This letter, containing the above, and other particulars, which I ſhall notice before I conclude, reached me on the 4th of Shabann (28 Auguſt) and afforded me great pleaſure.

"It is univerſally allowed, that there is nothing in the world more excellent than friendſhip and harmony, which are bleſſings to mankind in general. The maintainance of every article of the treaty, is equally incumbent on both parties.——It is not ſtipulated in any article of the treaty, that either party may ſend forces through dominions of the other, without conſulting him beforehand, and cauſe trouble and diſtreſs

to

to the people.——To what rule of friendship can be attributed the stationing of garrisons in the forts, and making collections in the country of the other party.—— *What has happened, is then agreeable to English faith.* In proof of this assertion, be it observed, that Colonel Leslie, the Commanding Officer of the detachment, has kept with him Ragonaut-Row's Vakeel, and, in conjunction with him, collects money from the dominions of the government, by intimidating its subjects.——This being the case, what becomes of your assurances before recited, that the treaty should be scrupulously adhered to, on your parts, so long as it was maintained by my master? or what degree of credit can be given thereto?

"From time immemorial, no forces of the maritime European nations, have marched by land through the dominions of the government: but the route of all the trading and European nations has been by the ocean. Nor is it stipulated in the treaty, that the English detachments shall have a passage through the government territories. Reflect maturely on this, and then determine, on whose side the blame rests.——— That such unlooked-for acts should proceed from you, is a matter of the highest astonishment; to think that mighty and powerful Chiefs should act in direct opposition to the faith of their engagements.——You are pleased to write, that if the Presidency of Bombay, shall still continue to require the troops, you can in no case, agree to recall them.——The matter is briefly thus.——The King of England, and the English Company, have placed confidence in the Supreme Council of Calcutta, and invested it with authority over all the other settlements. The acts of the Council of Calcutta are binding on the government of all the Company's settlements. Having given
this

this assurance, he proposed the form of a treaty, such as the critical situation of the times rendered necessary.—You transmitted a treaty conformably thereto, under the seal of the English Company.——It was from the beginning, the earnest wish of the government of Bombay, that no friendly connections should be established between the two states, and have been, ever since, striving to overset it. And notwithstanding the conclusion of the treaty, they kept Ragoba with them. How then, was it to be expected, that they should recall their troops, which were disturbing the peace of the government dominions? It even appears, to a conviction, that they persuaded Ragoba to the measures he has pursued. How then does the supreme authority of the Council of Calcutta from the King of England appear, since the Chiefs of the different settlements, do not regard engagements made by you, as binding on them, but make no scruple to break them; And you, Sir, paying no regard to your own acts, take your measures on the representations of the government of Bombay. This is indeed astonishing to the highest degree!

It is the dictate of sound policy that you withdraw your troops to your own territory. This will be a convincing proof of the sincerity of your friendship, and will spread the fame of your good faith, throughout the universe.

From the commencement of the government of the family of the Paishwa, they have entered into treaties with many of the Chiefs of the East and West, and have never before experienced such a want of faith from any one; nor, ever to the present time, deviated from their engagements, or been wanting to the duties of friendship and alliance; the blame rests with you.

The

The pacific difposition of the Maratta Court, and their refufal to treat effectually with St. Lubin, will appear from the following paffage in a letter from the Governor's friend, the Rajah of Berar.

A. No. VII.

I formerly intimated in my letters to Calcutta, the purport of what the Poonah Minifters wrote to me, That they neither had, nor would have, any friendfhip or connection with the French nation; and that the French agent came to Poonah, folely for the purpofes of trade; and that out of friendfhip to the Englifh they had fent him away; that I fhould therefore write to the Nabob Amand-ul-Dowla, (meaning the Governor General) to be perfectly fatisfied with refpect to them, they being fteady to their engagements.

The Out Lines of the Rohilla War.

THE extensive rich provinces called Rohil-cund, inhabited by a nation distinguished under the appellation of the Rohilla's, is placed, for the most part, in that beautiful and fertile site which extends between the two great rivers, Ganges and Jumna, from the boundary of Corah to the confines of Agra and Delhi; it occupies a large district of country on the North side of the Ganges, reaching Eastward to the Provinces of Oude, and to uninhabited mountains Northward; and it crosses the Jumna between Agra and Delhi. The revenues, without oppression, exceeded two Crores of Rupees annually, (two millions English) and their military establishment of cavalry and infantry, were about eighty thousand; a brave warlike race. The body of the people were composed of Hindoos, of a stature, complexion, constitution, and disposition, infinitely superior to those of the lower countries; but the fate of war procured to a set of martial Patan Mahomedans, an absolute dominion under the denomination of Chiefs or Rajahs. As they were numerous, single chiefships were not powerful, but united as branches sprouting from the same stock, and in a common cause, they were always deemed formidable.

These people lived on good terms with, and bore loyal attachment to the Emperor of Hindostan. The proximity of their Southern provinces, exposed them often to the ravages and depredatory incursions of the Marattas.

Marattas. To these depredations, may all their misfortunes be ascribed, which furnished a pretext to the aspiring ambition and restless impetuosity of Sujah-ul Dowla, the Vizier of the Empire, and Nabob of Oude, to usurp the dominion of a country, whose wealth, power, and vicinity would serve him as ascending steps to mount the Imperial Throne of Delhi. He artfully insinuated to the Rohilla Chiefs, that he was desirous to enter into an alliance with them, and to assist against the Marrattas, as a common enemy; but as they were to reap the chief benefit, it was proper that a subsidy should be paid for the services which his troops were to perform on remote expeditions. He had, previous to this measure, caused Mahomed Kouli Khan, the Nabob of Illiabad and Corah, to be basely assassinated when at his religious devotion, and then he usurped the dominion of his country, and thus brought his own provinces close home to those Rohilla provinces, which were the fields of plunder and rapine to the flying Marratta parties.

The Rohilla Chiefs, although they knew and suspected his general character, doubted not his sincerity on an occasion, which evidently accommodated himself, and they consented to pay Sujah-ul-Dowla forty Lacks of Rupees, if he would send a powerful army *immediately* to join their forces, in repelling, and driving the Marratta marauders out of their country. The Marratta's availing themselves of the Vizier's slow movements, and in the security which the promised succours from the Vizier had created in the Rohilla Chiefs, even to a relaxation of the necessary precaution, renewed their incursions and depredations with redoubled fury and alacrity, and with too much success; so that the Company's troops under the command of Sir Robert Barker, on the part of the Vizier, only entered the Rohilla country, for its defence, after all the mischief had been irretrieveably perpetrated. The Rohilla Chiefs were, by that means, so reduced in their finances, that besides mildly stating the non-performance of contract by Sujah-ul-Dowla, they were obliged by necessity to desire a respite in the complete payment of what he would be found to have any equitable claim to, by periodical installments, and proposed to make the presidency of Fort William the sole judges thereof; as all overtures were refused, they at length yielded to the measure of paying the whole original specific sum, upon condition of accommodating them with such reasonable terms, suited to the reduced state in which the late Marrata incursions, and the Nabob's own dilatory observance of the treaty, had left their countries.

This was the indentical object of the Vizier's policy; and it is not inconsistent with his ambition, treachery, and brutality, to suspect and believe, that he had his emissaries amongst the Marrattas, to stimulate and excite them to commit the late depredation, upon a promise from him, that his armies, notwithstanding the treaty he had concluded with the Rohilla Chiefs, should not obstruct their operations, until the year following, imagining, as it happened, that the pleas of necessity and equity, on the part of the Rohilla Chiefs, would furnish him with pleas for instant hostility and extermination.

Matters were in this state of suspence, when Mr. Hastings and his Council, resolved on a Committee of Circuit to settle the revenues, adjust the administration of the Dewannee, and liquidate other commercial and revenue concerns in the provinces of Bengal and Bahar,

har, and with Sujah-ul-Dowla, about the middle of the year 1773. A rupture, artfully contrived, separated the Members of Circuit on the day of their departure from Calcutta, and it fell to the pre-concerted lot of Mr. Hastings *solo*, to tune the instrument, correct the musical measures, and harmonize the discordant faculties of the Vizier Sujah-ul-Dowla; The Governor repaired to Benaras, the field of action, charged with discretionary powers in relation to matters of trade, and adjustment of the subsidy. There were several Members of Council, Sir Robert Barker the Commander in Chief of the army, and several senior servants of the Company, either by appointment, or in suite, at that time, in Benaras. But secret deeds dislike the light; and upon the principles of the negociation between the Governor and the Vizier, it would have been impolitic and dangerous in the extreme, to have had assistants or witnesses. Sir Robert Barker, resented the indignity offered to his military and civil stations in the Company's service, and as a man of probity, who set a proper value on the faith and honor of his nation, reprobated the treaty, as unjust, and dishonourable, which appears upon the public minutes of Council after their return to Calcutta. The presence and names of these gentlemen were only made use of, to witness the execution, and interchangeable delivery of the *public* articles of the treaty, upon the 18th September 1773. There were others of a much more intricate nature, not proper to be promulgated, reserved for the influence which the Governor's return, and improved condition, to the presidency, could only bring to bear by his *real* presence in Council, the act of Council being found indispensible to give it efficacy.

By this *public* treaty, the Vizier was to be invested, (and immediately to poffefs, as an eftate in perpetuity,) with the Emperor's rights to the provinces of Illiabad and Corah, which had been folemnly fecured to him by feveral facred treaties in 1765, and ratified by the Company openly, and impliedly by the nation; for this bold conceffion, he was to give the Company forty lacks of Rupees, as a confideration for a perpetual revenue of 45 lacks, under a wife adminiftration; and the tribute of 26 Lacks to the Emperor, from the Nabobfhip of Bengal, was, by thefe two Contractors, declared to have been forfeited from the 28th February 1772, except two fums which the Vizier, and Nudjiff Cawn (a colleague on this occafion) pretended to claim as a private debt from the King to them, both amounting to £. 92,800 fterling.

The firft part of the *fecret* treaty which tranfpired, confufedly, cautioufly, and by piece-meal, feveral months thereafter, contained the barbarous and fhocking tragedy, which a Britifh Commander in Chief, and an army officered by Britifh fubjects, and paid by the Britifh Eaft India Company, were made to act, in maffacring and exterminating a whole nation, diftinguifhed in Hindoftan for many fuperior qualifications, and putting Sujah ul-Dowla in the full poffeffion of their country, he paying the Company for the inhuman ufe of thefe mercenaries, the paultry pittance, (in proportion to the annual revenue, and of the plunder) of 50 lacks of Rupees, (as a balfam to their wounded confciencies) by four annual inftallments.

It is not very confiftent, with human ideas to conceive, far lefs to believe implicitly, that Mr. Haftings could have formed fo firm and infuperable an attachment,

ment, or personal friendship for a prince whose character was universally obnoxious, a perfect stranger to him, and who had received into his bosom (joined with them as the Company's enemies) those persons who, not long before, had inhumanly and perfidiously butchered in cold blood, his own colleagues and most intimate friends and companions, the members of the Council of Patna, and others; his secret motives or gratifications are subjects of suspicion, but they are obscured beyond the reach of legal proof. Every virtue that can dignify humanity, were the wanton offerings to gratify the ambition and sanguinary thirst of the most savage of his species.§ He engaged deliberately in an unnatural, unprovoked,

---

§ That Sujah-ul-Dowla should have protected and befriended Cossim Alli Cawn and Sombro, the murderers of Messrs. Hay, Ellis, Chambers, &c. will not be a matter of surprize, after the simple relation of the two following anecdotes, out of a hundred more.———Captain H———r, who was in the Company's service, and also in the Vizier's, had a boat with some merchandize, stopped by the Revenue Officers, for want of the proper permit. Without suspecting any tragical consequence, he mentioned it to the Vizier.———He was awaked at middle-night, and the head of the Phouzdar, (chief Magistrate) of the district, presented to him in a basket. A circumstance which shocked Captain H———r to that degree, that he scarce recovered his spirits while in India.

Colonel G———d, hunting one day in Rohilcund, some villagers whose hogs were killed by the dogs, threw a stick at one of the dogs.———The Colonel came to Sir R. B———r's tent, where the Vizier was at breakfast, and accidently mentioned the trifling circumstance. The Vizier whispered to one of his attendants, and before the breakfast was over, the attendant returned and informed the Vizier, that the village was destroyed, and man, woman, and child, put to the sword.

provoked, cruel war, to destroy an unoffending, industrous people, to whom the same mercenary arms had yielded succour, and friendly relief the preceding year. He sacrificed the sacred inherent rights of the Emperor, to raise the Emperor's own servant and subject, by an act of open rebellion and high treason. He violated the solemn treaties, upon which all the claims to trade, and the territorial revenues, accorded to the Company and nation, are founded and established, to the same unwarrantable purposes. He withdrew the tribute, which constituted the sole legal and political consideration for the Company's pretensions to the Dewannee, and the rights of the British nation, without consulting with his constituents, or his council, and against a ratified treaty, and ceded the Emperor's own provinces of Illiabad and Corah, to the Emperor's own minister, a mere temporary officer, removeable at his pleasure.——He, even, with an assurance and indecency, scarce to be equalled, avows, that the unauthorized treaty of Benares, and the secret conditions, which were only known to the two negociators, and not even committed to paper, were, to all intents and purposes, binding and obligatory on the Company; and in particular, he asserted, that the general tenor of the treaty, implied a positive obligation on the Company, to secure the Musnud to Sujah-ul-Dowla *and his posterity*, in the undisturbed possession of the Nabobship of Oude, together with the countries usurped by the sacrilegious murder of Mahomed Kouli Khan, and the treaty of Benaras; although in the same breath he acknowledges, that at the time of making the concessions, he had declared to the Vizier, *That he was acting and consenting to measures against the peremptory orders of his superiors.*——All these are conceptions and concessions, of so extravagant and preposterous a nature,

ture, so foreign to the utmost extention of the Companys' power, and so shameful and inglorious to the British nation, that the iniquitous and inhuman purposes expressed in them, are sufficient, in the eye of reason, as well as law, to declare the whole null and void from the beginning; and that nothing less, than the vilest prostitution of trust could have produced such a treaty, or dared to avow so absurd and impudent a construction upon it.

"Mr. Hastings contrived, to bring the majority of his Council, to approve the *public* treaty; and his subsequent equivocations and sophistry in Council, concerning the *secret* conditions stipulated between the Vizier and himself, in relation to the conquest of the Rohilla-provinces, demonstrated beyond a doubt, that he thought them of a texture and complexion, not proper for public disquisition.——This allegation, as well as private considerations for the sacrifices in question, are pretty distinctly implied in the appointment of a Resident at the Vizier's Court, where none had before been deemed necessary, upon his own special motion, claiming, authoritatively, an independent right to appoint and recall the proposed Resident, of his own free will and mere motion; that such Resident shall be considered as his (the Governor's) *private agent* and correspond *only with him*.——Mr. Hastings's minutes and report upon the occasion, are to the following purpose, and nearly literal. "*That it was* "*my intention to convince the Vizier, that in his concerns,* "*with the Company, the immediate dependence was upon* "*the Governor alone, and to establish a direct correspon-* "*dence, between him and myself, without any interven-* "*tion.*"——Could Mr. Hastings have adopted a surer maxim or language, or asserted a stronger line of influence,

fluence, to obtain an Asiatic recompence?——
He then proposed, "To appoint a person for transacting such matters of correspondence and communication with the Vizier, as he, (the Governor) shall think proper to entrust to his management; and he offers it, *frankly*, as his opinion, that if the Board shall entrust him with the *sole nomination* of such a Resident, and the power of *recalling him whenever he pleases, it may be attended with good effects, but not otherwise*."—What construction can be put on such declarations, recorded on the Companys' own proceedings, but that the result of the visit to Sujah-ul-Dowla, had placed the author, beyond the reach and power of his employers?—The confidential instructions to the Resident, and the correspondence with him and Colonel Champion, corroborate these surmises in pretty direct terms. By the instructions to Mr. Middleton, the Resident, he expressly "forbids any European, whether English or not, civil or military, in or out of the Companys' service, on any pretext, to visit the Vizier, or the Rajah Cheyt Sing, but particularly the Vizier; not even the European Officers in the Vizier's own service, except the Commander in Chief."——As Mr. Hastings obtained for the Rajah Cheyt-Sing, the Zemindary of the Provinces of Benaras Ghazipore, &c. *and to his posterity*, for 22¼ lacks of Rupees yearly rent, it may be supposed, that the son and heir of the rich Rajah Bulwant Sing, was also very liberal to his friend and benefactor; and therefore the prohibition to European visitors, was a necessary measure of prudent policy.——Mr. Hastings having written a *private* letter to Sujah ul Dowla, without any communication, as usual, through the Resident; the jealousy, or the fears of Mr. Middleton were roused, and he collected resolution enough to complain with some bitterness

terness of the flight and diffidence which it implied, in a letter to Mr. Hastings, dated the 4th June, 1774, wherein he says, "that having expressed his uneasi-
"ness to the Vizier, he was told by him, *that it was*
"*only a private complimentary letter.*"——And Colonel Champion, in a *private* letter to the Governor, before their quarrel, dated 30th May, 1774, uses these very suspicious and deep-meaning expressions.

"Dear Sir,
"In consequence of what passed between us at
"parting, I have mentioned Colonel Upton's claim to
"the Nabob, and requested he would be kind enough
"to discharge it. *His Excellency was very concise in his*
"*reply, that he had settled all money matters with Mr.*
"*Hastings.*"

What can be inferred from this, but that Mr. Hastings, had undertook to shut up all private claims and applications. And the reiterated strenuous endeavours, of Mr. Hastings, by uncommon application, and indirect insinuations, to prevail on Colonel Champion to dismiss from his service as Banyan, the very faithful and intelligent Collychurn, while upon the expedition, betrays a dread of his discovering, in the course of business, and negociations with the army, and at Lucknow, the secret springs which led to the treaty of Benaras. A Mr. Hall, whose address and management had procured him a general intercourse with the natives of condition, in and about the Vizier's court, and metropolis, having come down to Calcutta, somewhat involved, and finding no method to get extricated, bethought him of communicating the outlines of certain pieces of private knowledge, to a confidential friend of Mr. H   ; declaring that in his

his present distress, if he was not relieved, he must be under the necessity of laying his mind open to General Clavering: It had the intended effect, his debts were forthwith paid. But Mr. Hall *wisely* said, that he must have future subsistence, and more money for immediate use;—he received an order on Cossimbazar for present supply, and an appointment at Futtigur, upon express condition of going instantly, and remaining there, to execute it in person.

Colonel Champion was appointed to the command of the Company's troops, on an expedition, near 1500 miles by water conveyance up the country, against the Rohilla's, with peremptory orders to be directed in all his motions and actions by the Vizier, Suja-ul-Dowla, whose commands he was implicitly to obey on all occasions. The Colonel put himself accordingly, at the head of the army, and took the field, under the absolute command of a prince, whose object was savage barbarism and inhumanity, and who wanted manly courage to hazard, either his own person, his army, or even his artillery in action, to secure the success of what he was so solicitously ambitious to obtain.——— The fatal battle was fought, upon the 23d day of April, 1774, which iniquitously decided the melancholy fate of the brave, industrous, populous, and inoffensive Rohilla nation; at a time that Sujah-ul-Dowla, withdrew, with his army, artillery, and baggage, to a distance of several miles from the field of action:——Nay, he positively refused to the application of Colonel Champion, a part of his cavalry in order to attack the enemy at a certain quarter, to which the numbers of the Company's troops could not extend without imminent danger to the whole; and he also pointedly refused to spare a few pieces of his artillery, to serve in
another

another very necessary quarter. These refusals, created uneasy suspicions in Colonel Champion's mind, of foul treachery on the part of the Vizier, in case the success of the day favoured the Rohillas, which would place the vanquished army between a victorious enemy, and a treacherous friend. Such an idea might not be wanted to animate the British General, but it might have pushed him to a determined resolution, to conquer, or fall.— The Company's brave General and their troops, unassisted, gained a decisive, but in truth a disgraceful, victory. Their artillery were so judiciously stationed and pointed, that to the immortal honor of the brave Rohillas, it was asserted, they left 4000 men lying dead upon the field, before they retreated.

The surviving Chiefs, surrendered at discretion to the victorious army, and were delivered into the hands of Sujuh-ul-Dowla, except Fyzulla Cawn, who fled to the mountainous part of his country, by which means he was able to stipulate conditions, yielding up his camp and towns as plunder to the Vizier, but he could not, notwithstanding, obtain such other terms, as were consistent with either policy or humanity.—The other Chiefs were forced, together with their families, to submit to the most disgraceful imprisonment, and the most mortifying and humiliating treatment; their Zenanas, which are sacred sanctuaries in India, even against the violences and outrages of savages, were plundered, and the wives, daughters, and sisters of princes were violated and abused. Children under puberty were sacrificed to the lust of an old distempered debauchee., Some shocking circumstances have been alledged.———The plunder received into the possession of the Vizier, has been estimated at a crore and a half of Rupees, or 1,500,000£. sterling; and yet to this hour, or the beginning

ginning of the current year, 1780, 29 lacks.60,608 Rupees, part of the subsidy due for this conquest, are yet owing to the Company, besides ten Lacks promised as a donation to the army, in lieu of the plunder, which he had treasured to his own use.

It is conjectured, that about 500 thousand industrious husbandmen and artists, who were also, for the most part, able warriors, together with their families, were deliberately driven, openly, over the Jumna, to receive an asylum from their late enemies and plunderers, the Marrattas.——Fyzulla Cawn was obliged to condition, that he should not entertain more than 5000 persons under his dominion.——The latter end of 1777, under the vague pretence that Fyzulla's country was flourishing, and becoming more populous than was stipulated by treaty, Mr. Middleton, as the Company's Resident at Lucknow, in concert with his friends and protectors at the presidency, without any notification to the Supreme Board, or asking their consent, undertook to delegate Mr. Daniel Barwell, as an ambassador to the quiet, timid, Fyzulla Cawn, who, wrapt up in his garment of innocence, suspected nothing less than a charge of violating the compact, or the presence of an European ambassador, to adjust the imaginary violation. It is said, that although the allegation appeared to have been without foundation, the minister found the means of procuring, by way of escort back to Lucknow, several Elephants and Camels, loaded with eight to ten Lacks of Rupees in specie. The minute of Mr. Francis, upon the occacasion of the Governor General's motion, to approve the proceedings, as expedient, on the 9th March 1778, is worthy of the space it occupies upon record.

He,

He, (Mr. Francis,) calls it, "One of the grossest pieces of management he met with in India. Mr. Daniel Barwell quits his station at Benaras without leave, and goes to Lucknow without leave; Mr. Middleton instantly discovers, that Fyzulla Cawn is carrying on some design prejudicial to the interest of the Nabob, and that the Nabob gives cause for such designs, by his treatment of his subjects; at the same time, that nothing is more notorious, than that the Nabob, has no more power in his own country, than he (Mr. Francis) has. To put a stop to these effects, which mutual jealousies must produce, a treaty must be made, the guarantee of the Company must be given, and Mr. Daniel Barwell finds himself very opportunely, at Lucknow, ready to execute the commission."

The Rohilla Provinces are now a barren waste, and almost totally deserted by their remaining inhabitants. The Chiefs, or their children, are continued in the most miserable state of confinement, deprived of the common necessaries of life. As the proceedings of the Supreme Council in Calcutta, in 1775 and 1776, are printed, many of the particulars will appear in them, and in the letters of Colonel Champion, and other papers having relation to that barbarous measure. The remarker, having only his memory to recur to, is less perfect in the detail than he would wish to be, because the annals of that history require public investigation, by the nation whose arms stained its fame and glory, with indelible impressions, which cry aloud for justice, reparation, and exemplary punishment.

Narrative

Narrative of Proceedings in the Ordnance Department, and in the Office of Military Store-keeper.

AN accurate enquiry into the application of military stores, will bring peculations of magnitude into public view, either committed by direct authority, or under a collusion of high authority, which is the more dangerous in its consequences, by being less suspected. Military stores comprehend so large a portion of the Company's capital, that the Directors have long laboured to develope from the cloud of intricacies which obscured from their knowledge, the real value, as well as the regular expenditure and application thereof. To this judicious end, they pointedly instructed and enjoined their presidencies in India, and particularly in their several general letters to Bengal, under dates, 17th June, 1748, paragraphs 8 to 17 inclusive, 7th April, 1773, paragraph 4 and 5, and 7th January, 1774, paragraph 9. By these letters, the Company solemnly created the ostensible department of *military Store keeper*, on the abolition of, and to supercede the office of *gunner and gun-room crew*: the office to be executed by a *covenanted* servant,* who was to receive from the gunner, *and to retain in future in his actual possession and charge, and under his special care* (standing accountable out of his own private estate for all deficiencies) *all* the ordnance, carriages, arms, powder, shot, shells, tools, instruments, stores, and habiliments

of

---

* The limitation to a *covenanted servant* was clearly meant to preclude *military* officers from that trust.

of war whatsoever; *to have charge of the gun-room, and different magazines, and places where military stores were, or should be deposited;* with a special and peremptory injunction as to the mode of keeping the several books and accompts of his office, as well with respect to the receipts, and issues of all stores, having relation in any degree, to the service of war; whether at the presidency, or subordinate settlements, or on ship-board, transmitting copies annually, with explanatory observations, to the Court of Directors; and requiring obedience from him to the commands of the Governor and Council, who, only, should have authority to order the receipt and delivery of stores, after the *quality* † had been certified by the Major and next officer of artillery. Ordaining also, as a branch of the Store-keeper's duty, that he take care to prevent the stores receiving *avoidable* damage, and to keep them from time to time in repair; that stores appropriated occasionally for immediate expenditure, shall, *only*, be delivered to the seperate charge and custody of the *Director of the Labrotary* (now denominated *Commissary of stores.*) And that *all* applications for supplies, issues, and payments, shall pass through the military Storekeeper, to the Governor and Council, for their warrant to accomplish it.

To the same ends, and in proper obedience to the commands of the Court of Directors, it appears by a letter upon record, from Claud Russel, Esq; military Store-keeper to the commissary of stores, on the 26th July, 1768, that from a firm belief of abuses committed in

---

† The *quality* and not the *quantity* on *application*, is alone to be certified, this confirms the check intended to be invariably preserved, over the military interfering in a line, meant to be civil.

in the magazines by the embezzlement of stores, it was neceſſary to compell a ſtrict obſervance of the *eſtabliſhed regulation of the* military Store-keeper's office, which regulations were for ſimilar good purpoſes, and likewiſe to preſerve the conſtitutional authority, ſuper-intendency, and eſſential check of the Store-keeper (on the 24th January, and 10th February, 1774,) claimed and exerciſed by the Honourable Charles Stewart, the then military Store-keeper, in letters to the board of inſpection ; and effectually eſtabliſhed, by a reſolution of, and notice from the Board, to Mr. Stewart of the latter date; which he accordingly communicated officially, to the commiſſary of ſtores, on the 17th of the ſame month.

By a ſtudied violation of theſe wiſe, ſalutary, and poſitive inſtitutions, it may be made to appear, that ſtores, to a very conſiderable amount, have been deficient, and *commanded* to be *wrote off*, the expenditure of which doth not appear in any record; or any formal enquiry into the cauſes.¶ That the department created by the Court of Directors, to controul iſſues and diſburſements, and to be reſponſible for ſtores depoſited, is, *in effect*, aboliſhed, apparently for the purpoſe of abuſe, in all ſenſes, and by all means, with impunity.§ The oſtenſible office of Store-keeper, is rendered *ineffectual*, and

¶ See the Store-keeper's letter of October 1778, concerning cartouch-boxes, &c. and the deficiencies on the ſurvey in 1779, abſtracted in ſeveral minutes and letters in this narrative.

§ See the Governor General's minutes abſtracted throughout this narrtive, particularly in October 1778, 25th February, 8th July, and 19th Auguſt, 1779; and Colonel Watſon's of the 5th January 1780.

and declared *nominal*, by the heads of administration, while the sole power of indents, receipts, issues, and applications, is vested in the person, who, in the very terms of the consolidated charge, ought not to have it.* The Store-keeper, (*a covenanted civil servant*,) having neither the power of creating demands for supplies, nor to apply them when issued. Whereas, the Commissary, in whom *partiality*† has vested the accumulated power before mentioned, by holding also the second rank and command in the artillery corps, however fair and unexceptionable his conduct and character in private life, possesses in this public instance, the incompatable privilege or indulgence, of creating wants, indenting for supplies, furnishing many of them and their expenditure, if he chuses to exercise the complicated vestiture improperly.‡ The names and denominations of stores, and the mode of keeping the accompts were mutilated, seemingly for the purpose of perplexing, and to counteract the orders of the Directors, as the means of deception with facility, to cover

and

---

* See abstracts of the Governor's minutes, on the October 1778, 25th February, 8th July, and 19th July, 1779, and those of Mr. Francis, and Mr. Wheler in reply.

† The application of the word *partiality*, has been justified on many occasions. One instance may serve to judge of others by. Flints are rated in the Store-keeper's agency at 10 per thousand, and he had abundance ready to deposit when wanted; Colonel Green, the Commissary was nevertheless contracted with, and he supplied them into store, at the advance price of 49 Rupees per thousand.

‡ See abstracts from Mr. Francis and Mr. Wheler's minutes, of 8th July, and 19th August 1779.

and disguise deficiencies. § The Store-keeper was ordered to desist from keeping books in his office, which constituted an essential branch of the check over receipts and expenditures, and at last he was stripped of the only remaining, and equally essential controul, which a joint lock and key with the Commissary, gave him over the stores.* Positive orders, and pointed instructions were infracted, and disobeyed with contempt, and the contempt attempted to be justified upon the Companys' own record.† In-direct menaces, and insinuations of dismission, were uttered in terrorem, to prevent the faithful discharge of public duty, and obstruction to favorite, but destructive measures.‡ Arms fit for *actual service*, and others *reparable*, were sent out of store (at a period of danger, and when the arsenal was very incomplete) as totally *unserviceable*, without survey, or the authority of the controuling Board, and without the knowledge or concurrence of the military Store-keeper.§ *Serviceable* arms were in like manner converted into ship's kentledge, and rendered for ever *unserviceable*.‖

These

---

§ See Companys' records, Board of Ordnance, observations by the Secretary on the survey, and the Store-keeper's explanations.

* See the subsequent abstracts in this narrative.

† See abstracts from minutes in this narrative.

‡ See the abstracts of minutes by Mr. Hastings, the 8th July, 19th August, and September, 1779, in the subsequent narrative.

§ See abstract from Mr. Livius letter, 27th November, 1779.

‖ See the letters of Mr. Secretary Auriol, Mr. Livius, and Mr. Petrie.

These censures, being of a serious nature, call for some evidence to secure a degree of faith, if not according to the very strict letter and practice of the courts of law in all cases, at least to carry ample conviction to the minds of the public. With this view, however tedious it may prove in the recital, the only doctrine proposed, will be abstracted from the Companys' own records, which will at the same time serve as a concise narrative of the strange proceedings, on a subject so materially important to the English East India Company.

The general letters recited at the beginning of this enquiry, (1748, 1773, and 1774,) shew the principles on which the military Store-keeper's department was constituted, distinguish the official duty and responsibility of the officer, direct the mode of keeping the books and accompts of his office, and apply injunctions concerning *reparable and irreparable stores*.

By a regulation of the Board of Ordnance, the 17th June, 1775, to prevent inconveniences and impediments *in the emission of daily stores*, the charge and responsibility of such, *as the Commissary should indent for, and receive from the Store-keeper for the use of the Commissary's office*, shall be vested in the Commissary *alone*, being accountable to the Store-keeper, &c. for the application and expenditure of them.*

In the proceedings of the Board of Inspection, on the 25th September, 6th November, and 19th December

---

* See the proceedings previous to this resolution in 1748, 1773, and 1774.

ber, 1777, &c. it appears, that upon Mr. Hasting's motion, the orders of the Court of Directors, in relation to the military Store-keeper's office and duty, are annulled, without a plea of propriety or expediency to justify the measures. He is particularly commanded to desist from keeping a journal and ledger. The Store-keeper having, in discharge of duty, used the freedom to make judicious representations with deference and delicacy on the 28th November, the subject thereof was referred on the 9th December, to the Accomptant General for his opinion.

On the 22d January following, the Accomptant General reported in support of the Store-keeper's reasoning. The impropriety and inexpediency of *unnecessary* disobedience, influenced the majority to yield, upon this occasion, to the arguments of the minority, and the Store-keeper was permitted to resume the use of a journal and ledger in his office. The Board again referred to the Accomptant General for a more perfect form of keeping the books of the Ordnance and Storekeeper's offices, in greater conformity with each other, by having the same denomination to the principal accompts.

October 1778. The military Store-keeper, as a member of the Board of Ordnance, entered a minute and motion, *concerning deficiencies unaccounted for*, and positively refusing, without an order of council, to comply with the resolution of that Board, *by writing off, as if expended on service,* 3500 cartouch boxes, and divers other articles, *said* to be lost or deficient, which could not be made appear to have been expended; representing the loose and imperfect state of the Storehouses and stores, without check or controul; and

therefore

therefore, in order to obviate all future deficiencies, in-correctnesses, and difficulties, he moved, that a survey of all stores, now in store, be made, in order to correct the books with the goods actually exifting, and balance the deficient accounts by opening another account under the denomination of profit and lofs, with the confent, and by the exprefs authority of the Governor and Council; and in order that in future the Store-keeper shall (as in Europe) be refponfible for all effects committed to his charge.

Proceedings of the Board of Infpection, 17th December 1778, with the Accomptant General's plan for keeping the accounts of the military Store-keeper; and the proceedings of the Board of Ordnance. The Board ordered a furvey in terms of the Store-keeper's motion on the   October at the Board of Ordnance, to be completed on the 30th day of April following: and that the books of the fubordinate departments be corrected and adjufted in conformity to the ftores which shall actually be then afcertained in ftore. And that a like annual furvey fhall be made on the 30th of April. Upon this occafion Mr. Haftings, in an elaborate minute, difcovers his views, a partiality to the Commiffary of ftores, and inclination to fuppref the controul of the military Store-keeper, and he committed this fingular declaration upon record, thus, " *I am myfef lefs* " *folicitous about the books of the military Store keeper,* " *as they are now either totally ufelefs, or ufeful only as* " *checks on the receipts and iffues of the Commiffary of* " *ftores.*" It merits peculiar attention, that the Commiffary over whom this " *totally ufelefs check*" is acknowledged to be held, is the perfon in whofe province it is to receive and appropriate moft of the ftores iffued, and to indent for, as well as to furnifh by contract

tract and agency, a considerable part of them. Another fact equally notorious in this minute is, that the Governor-General is either totally unacquainted with the nature of accounts and the forms of book-keeping, or that he openly meant, by an exertion of a temporary power, to remove all controul from such persons as he might favour in future, as well as to cancel past transgressions, however injurious to the interests of his employers, and dangerous to their existence in Asia.

Mr. Wheler's reply to the Governor's minute, while it discovers a steady and faithful attachment to the duties of the trust reposed in him, shews him also to have a clear idea of books and accounts, as well as of the real spirit of the orders of the Court of Directors, and the utility, as well as necessity, of so sensible a controul throughout the several civil and military departments; and generally approved the mode of the Store-keeper's books, as essential for those purposes, although still capable of further improvement.

The proceedings of the Board of Inspection, 25th February, 1779, with a letter from the military Storekeeper, dated 23d current, complaining that the Commissary of stores had refused obedience to the order of the Board, for affixing a lock and key to the storerooms according to custom, because, " *That the receipts and issues of stores in the department, are not regulated by any particular time of the day.*" The Store-keeper justifies the complaint upon principles equally consistent, irrefutable, and official. The refusal on the other part, with the subsequent language of Mr. Hastings, in vindication and support of the Commissary's independence, favour strongly of a collusion incompatable with their respective duties to the Company.

Company. The Governor proposes, with a singularity peculiar only to his own sagacity, impenetrable (he supposes) to all others, " That each store-house " shall be *separately* surveyed, and that *during the ex-* " *amination*, the military Store-keeper may place his " key upon the *particular* store-house, *immediately* under " examination, *and instantly thereafter to be taken off.*"

Thus, according to Mr. Hastings's mode of survey, if it was necessary to conceal deficiencies, nothing could be more easy and simple than to remove stores from the store-houses already surveyed, into any other that remained to be surveyed, as the Commissary possessed *all* power except over that *immediately under examination*. It is astonishing, that the open falacy of such a measure, did not occur, even to the authors, as it could not possibly escape their opponents, although delicacy may have restrained the application by language to defeat it.

The Governor in a subsequent minute on the same day, in reply to Mr. Wheler and Mr. Francis, obstinately persists in the measure, and says, " That " he objects to Mr. Wheler's motion, requiring two " locks to be continued on each store, as well *after* " as *during* the examination, *i. e.* the Store-keeper's " lock, and the Commissary's lock, as mutual checks, " because, (the Governor alledges) the motion of Mr. " Wheler is made without a reference to the reasons " which induced the Board to place the super-inten- " dancy in the fort, under the immediate charge of " the Commissary of stores ; and because he considered " Mr. Livius (the military Store-keeper) as in effect
" a con-

" *a contractor for stores, and not Store-keeper,* although
" that title be still allowed him *of courtesy.*"

Mr. *Wheler,* in answer to the governor's *first* minute,
moved " for the survey of each appartment *separately,*
" and that the military Store-keeper, and commissary of
" stores should *severally* entertain locks and keys on
" *each* appartment, as well *after,* as *during* the *intire*
" examination, agreeably to the original establishment
" of the two offices. *i. e.* That the two locks and keys
" be kept upon each Store-room; one key to be kept
" by the Commissary's Circar*, and one by the mili-
" tary Store-keepers."

Mr. *Francis* concured in opinion with Mr. Wheler,
and added, " that the military Store-keeper was the
" natural and official check over the expenditure of
" stores by the Commissary. That he had uniformly
" disapproved very much of removing that check, by
" depriving the military Store-keeper of a lock and
" key upon the stores, as other methods might have
" been taken to facilitate the dispatch of business, sup-
" posing the joint trust to have been a cause of some
" occasional delay therein."

And in reply to Mr. Hastings's second minute,
Mr. *Francis* says, " that the alteration in question (or-
" dering the *temporary* application of a second lock and
" key) was made by the Board of Ordinance, which
" had not the authority to repeal an alteration made by
" government. That he could not agree, that the in-
" dulgence allowed the military Store-keeper, and to
" the

---

* By *Circar* is meant, a *Hindoo writer.*

"the other heads of offices to supply a part of the stores
"in their respective departments, vacated their offices.
"That if the military Store-keeper had any concern in the
"expenditure of the stores, the indulgence would have been
"highly improper. He had none. But as the military
"Store-keeper ought to have a check upon that person who
"has the expenditure of the stores, and over whom there is
"at present no controul. That with respect to the supply
"of stores, by the heads of offices, and by the military
"Store-keeper in particular, it was a measure strongly
"recommended by the Governor General himself,
"for reasons which did then, and do now appear
"to him (Mr. Francis) to be solid and un-
"answerable."

Mr. Wheler, in further reply to the Governor General's second minute, desired, "That the resolution
"of the Board of Ordnance, the 17th June 1775, be
"entered, in order to shew, that the responsibility of
"such stores *only* as the Commissary shall in future
"indent for, be intrusted to him *alone*. Hence, he
"concluded, that stores not indented for, and not
"immediately in demand, were to remain in the
"arsenal, under the united charge of the Commissary,
"and the military Store-keeper. That he was con-
"vinced the resolution would go no farther, and on
"that ground only, would he accede to it. That he,
"at the same time, maintained the propriety of his
"former proposition, *i. e.* that all stores, not falling
"under that description, be again returned to the
"charge of both offices."

The Governor General and *Mr. Barwell*, having three votes between them, carried in favor of the Governor's motion, and the Commissaries independance,

dance, and absolute power over all the Ordnance and military stores whatsoever.

Proceedings at the Board of Inspection on the 8th of July 1779. The *Governor General* expressed in pointed terms, his fixed dissatisfaction at the pretensions of the minority in support of the military Store-keeper's right to controul the Commissary of stores and his determined purpose, not to suffer, under any pretence, the check constitutionally established in the military Store-keeper, by the custody of another key on the store-houses; in the course of his opposition, he advances as a new doctrine, " *That the title* " *of military Store-keeper, which Mr. Livius originally* " *bore, with the actual charge implied by it, but which* " *from a tenderness to him has been suffered to remain,* " *although the charge was removed, has furnished him* " *with grounds for various pretensions. That in effect,* " *he is not the military Store-keeper. The only substantial* " *connexion that he has with that office, by any appointment* " *of the Board is as a contractor for stores, and in that* " *character, he is the last person in the service, whom* " *the Board should chuse to be a check upon the* " *Commissary.*"

Let it be decided by any disinterested person, whether Major Green, to whom the stores are issued *in his military capacity*, who indents for, and expends the stores *in the military capacity*, and who is also a *contractor* for, and *manufacturer* of many capital articles, is not less qualified to act as a Commissary, than Mr. Livius, (simply a civil covenanted servant) is to act as a Storekeeper? and whether the Governor's insinuations, do not directly tend to intimidate Mr. Livius from the due exercise of the duties and claims inherent in his office, to avoid the threatned dismission?

Proceedings at the Board of Inspection, on the 19th August 1779. The *Governor* continues to pursue his favorite maxim, of favoring his favorites, against all opposition, and by all manner of means, with a vehemence and warmth, which denounced dismission and vengeance on those, whose probity and fidelity were accidentally thrust as stumbling-blocks to obstruct the rapidity of his career.

The Governor acquaints the Board, " That he was " this morning informed by the Commissary of stores " that he had delivered his report to the Board of " Ordnance, and that Mr. Livius's locks *still* re- " mained affixed to the store-rooms. That he, there- " fore, moved, *that Mr. Livius be peremptorily or-* " *dered to remove them*; *and that the sole charge of* " *the store-rooms be left with the Commissary of* " *stores.*"

The Commander in Chief, *Sir Eyre Coote,* agreed to the Governors motion.

Mr. *Wheler* referred the Board to the positive injunctions contained in the general letters of 17th June, 1748, 7th April 1773, and 7th January, 1774.———— Observing in conclusion, " *how impossible it will be* " *for the Store-keeper to comply with their order,* " *if the keys which constitute this trust are delivered* " *solely to the charge of another*; *but that if the* " *Board think proper to set aside, both the orders of the* " *Court of Directors, and the regular official plan of*

carrying

" *carrying their orders into execution, they must answer*
" *the consequences.*"

The *Governor General*, in reply, minutes "thus,
" whatever the Company's orders may prescribe in this
" case, however necessary it may be, that the Store-keeper
" should have a joint charge of the stores with the Com-
" missary, still it would be highly improper upon the pre-
" sent occasion, to allow it in disobedience to a positive
" order of the Board, which must first be repealed, before
" such a regulation can take place."§—The Governor
again stiles Mr. Livius, "*The contractor of stores, for
" he is no Store-keeper,*" And in addition to his former
motion, he desires, " that *Mr. Livius may be called upon
" again, to inform the Board of the reasons why his locks
" are still upon the store-rooms. And that when the Board
" shall have received his answer, they will then judge,
" whether he has, or has not, been guilty of a disobedience
" of their orders.*"

Mr. *Francis* observed, " that the military Store-
" keeper had not (in his idea) disobeyed the orders of
" the Board, because it does not appear that he could
" have obeyed them sooner."

Mr.

---

§ How severely the Governor lashes himself whose disobedience, and repeated violation of orders, set the dangerous
example to all the inferior servants? Does not the same argument
hold more powerfully against the violation of the orders of the
Court of Directors, by the establishment of the order in question,
without waiting for the repeal of the original order in Leaden-
hall-street.

Mr. *Wheler* declared, that he would not justify any irregularity against the Orders of the Board. He finishes a very sensible and faithful minute, in these words, " *If, as the Governor-General says, Mr. Livius is the Contractor of stores, and no Store-keeper, by the same propriety of argument, Major Green, acting likewise in the character of a Contractor, has as little pretentions to the sole charge of the stores, and has as little right to the title of Commissary of stores, as Mr. Livius has to that of military Store-keeper.*

The *Governor-General's* minute, in September 1779, in council, on the subject of Mr. Belli's contract for victualling Fort William, gave birth to fresh charges and insinuations against, and investigations of the office of military Store-keeper. Although the contract under consideration did not bear the most remote affinity, or similitude in any sense whatever, to the military Store-keeper's appointment and duty, yet the Governor having the unperishable seed of resentment implacable on the one side, and partiality on the other, sowed in a fertile mind, levelled a most illiberal, and unjust blow at Mr. Livius, and through him at Mr. Francis, in these violent terms.. " *Mr. Livius has an Agency, with* 15 *per cent on articles rated by former charges of Commissaries, of course, greatly above the real cost.*" And in continuation, he adds, " *Mr. Livius is professedly patronized by Mr. Francis, who passes his bills, and nine or ten Lacks paid to him, are yet unaccounted for.*"

On this occasion Mr. Hastings's Indian moderation abandoned him, or he wittingly yielded the truth a sacrifice, to convict himself of a falshood; and in special terms avowed his own infidelity, in the discharge

charge of the public duty, in order to intimidate, and deter the opponents to one of his destructive favorite measures. He consented to give a commission of 15 *per cent.* on stores, which he ingenuously acknowledges, were charged by the Agent, "*greatly above the real* "*cost.*" Thus admitting, that besides a very high advantage upon the purchase, the Agent was to have a commission of 15 per cent, not upon the real cost, or purchase price, but upon the cost and advance, conjointly.

Mr. *Francis* procured, both for himself and the Store keeper, ample satisfaction in the sequel, which forced Mr. Hastings to *retract* his malignant declaration, and to minute the retraction upon the face of a public record.

Mr. *Francis* having been absent for health, when Mr. Hastings rashly charged him with conniving in Mr. Livius's *imaginary* peculations, and the *possession of large sums unaccounted for*. He replied to that part of the Governor's minute by letter, dated Houghly the 2d of October, 1779, thus, "the Governor "General's minute was transmitted to me this morning. "If recrimination does not imply an admission of the "charge, it certainly is no defence against it. I "cannot allow that one abuse is justified by another. "Nor am I bound to answer any objections, whether "valid or not, to the Agency of stores held by Mr. "Livius.—The Governor General and Mr. Barwell, "had just as much concern in giving it to him, as I "had.——If it be liable to abuse, why is it not cor- "rected? If his profits have been too great, why have "they not been reduced? Mr. Hastings and Mr. "Barwell have had absolute power in their hands for
"three

" three years.—It is said, that Mr. Livius has an
" Agency, with 15 per cent, or articles rated by former
" charges of Commissaries, of course greatly above the
" real cost.—If the assertion were true in terms, it
" remains to be explained, even on the principle of
" precedents, how the giving 15 per cent to one agent,
" justifies the giving 30 per cent to another. Messieurs
" Robinson, Kilican, and Crofts, reported that twenty
" per cent per annum, would be a reasonable commission
" to Mr. Belli. Mr. Hastings and Mr. Barwell, ne-
" vertheless gave him thirty.—With respect to the mili-
" tary Store-keeper's book of rates, the fact is, that
" it was formed by the late Colonel Dow with the ap-
" probation of the Board of Ordnance ; *not by the*
" *former charges of the Commissaries,* but by an enquiry
" into the actual Bazar prices of that period. Whether
" Mr. Livius gains or loses by these rates, is unknown
" to me; I believe that occasionally he may do both,
" nor does it concern the service in question". It is
said, " that Mr. Livius is professedly patronized by
" me." I recommended him to the office of military
" Store-keeper, and I will maintain him in the just
" right belonging to it, *on the same principles on which*
" *I would insist on his performing the duties of it.* Thus
" far my patronage of Mr. Livius had extended."

" But it is now said, *that I pass his bills*, the asser-
" tion as it stands expressed, may be supposed not to
" be a mistake. The Governor well knows that I
" resigned the employment of *Comptroller of the Offices*,
" from the end of December 1778 ; and that I have
" repeatedly urged to him the necessity of requesting
" some other Member of the Board, to undertake it
" from that period. Places of influence and profits,

" are not often so easily relinquished.* If the ac-
" counts of the public offices, have not since been ex-
" amined, the Governor General, I presume, will
" assign his reasons for it to the Company. Neither
" is it true, that I even passed Mr. Livius's bills
" in the sense plainly implied by the Governor.
" They were constantly examined by Mr. Baugh and
" his assistant, with the utmost strictness, before they
" came to me for their final confirmation. My diary
" is before the Court of Directors. It was not possi-
" ble therefore, that I could favor Mr. Livius, or
" any body else, unless Mr. Baugh and I acted in col-
" lusion. I desire that he may be examined at the
" Board, upon his oath, and in my absence, concerning
" the manner in which I executed my part of the exa-
" mination; and I most earnestly request of Mr.
Wheler

---

* to shew the jealousy of power, and the evils consequential thereof, the following detail will evince. Mr. Francis, *as youngest Member of Council*, had been nominated from the beginning, to examine the accounts of contractors, agents, offices, and general disbursements, and to controul all expenditures whatever, under the denomination of *comptroller of the offices*, which duty he regularly performed weekly. Sometime after the appointment and arrival of Mr. Wheler, whose official duty, *as youngest Member*, it then became, Mr. Francis then relinquished it at Christmas 1778, and moved at the board to name the successor. His resignation was received, but no successor appointed. In about a month he renewed the motion, it was slighted. In a further time, he proposed the nomination of Mr. Wheeler, *as youngest Member*, it was once again neglected. And upon a fourth peremptory proposition to the same effect, it was objected to by Mr. Hastings, with a frank avowal, " *that it was conferring too popular a power in an individual,*" and it was over-ruled. In which state the disbursements still continue, without any controul or examination, not even by the whole board.

" Wheler to make a motion in my behalf to this ef-
" fect, at the next Board of Inspection. I will leave
" it to Mr. Hastings and Mr. Barwell, to put such
" questions to him as they think fit. It would be
" much beneath me to make any other reply to the
" conclusion evidently meant to be drawn from the
" supposed fact, *of my passing Mr. Livius's bills,* but
" that I receive it as it deserves.

"　Again it is asserted, " *That nine or ten Lacks, thus
" paid to Mr. Livius, are yet unaccounted for.* I do not
" know what the amount of the Military Store-
" keeper's disbursements may be since December last,
" having no concern in the examination of his ac-
" counts. The Secretary has the monthly accounts
" before him, and I desire he will state the amount,
" during that period, in this place, (by the secretary it
" was filled up,) current Rupees 4 lacks, 13,965,13,6
" the Military Store-keeper's accounts of his disburse-
" ments being given in to him, every month,
" and a balance struck before he receives a further
" allowance for the ensuing month. It cannot truly
" be said, that the sums he received since December
" last, are unaccounted for. If his accounts are not
" examined, it is not his fault.

"　Any person unacquainted with the transaction of
" business in the Military Store-keeper's office, and
" who saw only in what circumstances, and with
" what apparent view, it is asserted, that 9 or 10 Lacks
" thus paid to Mr. Livius since December last, are
" yet unaccounted for, would naturally conclude, that
" this money was all on account of his agency, for
" the provision of Military Stores. For if it were
" not so, the comparison between his supposed profits,
"　　　　　　　　　　　　　　　　　　　　　" and

"and those of Mr. Belli, (to shelter which, Mr. Livius's name, and office, are manifestly introduced) proves nothing, and falls to the ground. Now the fact is, that the greatest part of the monthly sums issued to Mr. Livius, are advanced to him *as Military Store-keeper*, not as *agent*. Out of these he pays his own office charges *by a fixed establishment*; the *establishment* of the Commissary's Office; with the price of all the articles furnished by Lieutenant Colonel Green *by contract*; the price of all the powder furnished monthly, by the *powder Contractor*; and many other contingencies. In the management of all these disbursements, the Military Store-keeper pays as fast as he receives, and has no profit whatsoever, not even that of having a sum of public money for a short time in his hands. It is a fact, not unworthy of notice in this place, that all the other heads of offices receive their monthly advances, twenty days before the Military Store-keeper does, owing to some difficulty of adjustment, between him and the Commissary, by which in this respect, they both suffer."

"The following settlement, which I have desired the Secretary to fill up, will show what proportion the foregoing disbursements bear to the total amount of advance to the Military Store-keeper since December last."

1. Total

		R	A	P
1. Total amount of advance to the Store-keeper, from January 1779, inclusive. Current Rupees		4,42,105	7	6
2. Amount of Military Store-keeper's office charges *per* establishment		6,899	8	
3. Amount of money paid to Lieutenant Colonel Green, for charges of office, and for supplies.		16,321	7	8
4. Amount of the Powder Contractor's bills paid.		1,24,605	15	9
5. Amount of all other contingent charges paid.		1,22,116	2	10
Disbursements, without benefit to the Storekeeper.		2,69,943	1	3
Difference being for supplies by the Storekeeper.		1,72,162	6	3	4,42,105	7	6

In consequence of a motion sent in circulation by Mr. Wheeler, at the request of Mr. Francis, Mr. Baugh attended the Council Board on the 1st November 1779. The Governor-General declined to put questions in the mode prescribed, thinking it irregular, and alledging, that so *unimportant* did he consider Mr. Francis's last minute, which regarded three capital offices very materially, " *that he had not even given it an* " *intire*

" *intire perusal, although he had it by him for some time.*"
Whereupon Mr. Wheeler, after expressing the disagreeable task, which the Governor's declining it, had put on him, of asking answers to some queries from Mr. Baugh, and then delivered the following questions.

Question 1*st*. " Whether it is not your duty, as assistant to the Comptroller of the offices, to examine the monthly accounts of each office, before they are seen by the Comptroller, and to furnish him with whatever remarks may have occurred to you thereon."

Answer, " Preparatory to the Comptroller's examining the accounts of the offices, they have always been examined by my assistant, so far as respected their calculation and addition; after which, they have been compared by me with the vouchers delivered with them. I have then compared such charges as were established, with the fixed establishments, also such charges for stores provided by contract, or by agency, with the terms of the different engagements for those supplies; and if upon this examination I have discovered any deviation from either, I gave pointed them out to the Comptroller, who has either immediately deducted the difference, or applied to the head of that department, whose accounts were under examination for an explanation."

Question 2*d*. " Whether you have not constantly done so?

* From 3d October to 1st November, being 29 days.

Answer

Answer. "Yes, I have."

Question 3d. "Whether you have ever observed, that Mr. Francis in examining the accounts of the Military Store-keeper, or of any other of the public offices, or in passing their bills, or in any other instance whatever, has favoured the Military Store-keeper, or any other person, or has ever suffered an error or overcharge in his or their accounts, to pass without correction and censure?"

Governor General. "I beg that Mr. Baugh may be dispensed from answering that third question. If there is a necessity for it, it is highly improper, on many accounts, considering the wide difference between Mr. Baugh and Mr. Francis, that he should be obliged to answer to such a question. *I do not recollect what words of mine have given occasion for it, but if I have made use of any, which either directly lay such a charge to Mr. Francis's account, or imply it, I retract them, without accounting at this time, for the manner in which any such expressions may have escaped me, as they are now intirely out of my memory. The object of the question therefore is removed.*

Mr. Francis. "I am satisfied; and desire the question may be waved."

Question 4th. "To what point of time, have the Military Store-keeper's accounts been examined, and passed by the Comptroller?"

Answer. "To the end of December 1778."

Question 5th. "What is the intire amount of the several monthly sums issued to him from the treasu-

" ry, for the disbursements of his office, including
" his agency since December, 1778, to the end of Sep-
" tember last."

Answer. " The advances made to the Military Store-
" keeper from the Treasury, between the 1st of Janu-
" ary, and 30th of September, 1779, amount to,
" current Rupees, 4,24,000, but in this sum, is not
" included, his advance on account of September, be-
" ing 42,000 Rupees, because it did not pass the
" Board in time to be issued during that month. The
" order on the Treasurer was not signed 'till the 30th
" of September; and I observe by the estimate of the
" Store-keeper's disbursements for October, that the a-
" mount was not received 'till the 6th of the last men-
" tioned month. In Mr. Francis minute of the 2d.
" October, the amount of the advances issued to the
" Military Store-keeper to the end of August, is stated
" by me at current Rupees, 4,42,195:7:6, but it is
" proper to remark, that in this sum is included the
" monthly payments made to him by Mr. Robert
" Stuart, on account of the new powder works, and
" his receipts for ready money sales."

Question 6th. " Has the Military Store-keeper deli-
" vered in his monthly accounts regularly to the
" Comptroller's office, since December last?"

Answer. " Yes, to the end of September.

Governor General. " I desire to put the two follow-
" ing questions to Mr. Baugh."

1st. " Have Mr. Livius's accounts ever appeared
" before the Board?

2d. " What

" 2d. " What is the amount of Mr. Livius's receipts
" and disbursements, from the time he first had charge
" of the present office, to the date of my minute in
" September?

" If Mr. Baugh cannot answer the last of these questi-
" ons from his own official knowledge, I desire him
" to obtain proper official information to compleat his
" answer.

Answer to the Governor's 1st Question.

" They never have appeared before the Board. It
" was not the intent of the regulation, constituting the
" Comptroller's office, that they should be laid before
" the Board."

Ditto to the 2d.

" Not having the necessary materials in my possession
" for furnishing the account required by the Governor-
" General, I applied for it to the Military Store-
" keeper, and beg leave to lay before the Board, the
" following Abstract, which I have in consequence
" received from him, of his receipts and disbursements,
" from April, 1775, to September, 1779, inclusive."

" The receipts amounting to, current Ru-
" pees, - - 23,16,074:13:3
" The disbursments, to - - 23,16,783: 1.3

" Balance advanced by, and due } - 708: 4:
" to the Store-keeper,* - }

" Mr.

---

* This balance of 708 Rupees and 4 Annas in favour of the Military Store-keeper, differs materially from Mr. Hastings's charge of his having nine or ten lacks of Rupees in his hands, unaccounted for.

"Mr. Livius was appointed to the office of Military Store-keeper, on the 20th of March, 1775, and the Governor's Minute is dated in September, 1779.

"I think it proper to acquaint the Board, that my application for this account, would have been made to the Accomptant General, and not to the Military Store-keeper, could the former have finished it complete. But the General Books, being balanced only to the 30th of April, 1778, it could not have been prepared from them to a period subsequent to that time. I believe also, that the Entries in the General Books, are adjusted from the Abstracts of the receipts and disbursements supplied to the Accomptant-General, by the heads of the different Offices."

To shew, as well the truth of the facts alledged in their deepest colours, as their dangerous consequences, throughout the deliberate train of abuses: Two recent transactions carry an aspect, which unite the links to render the chain of circumstances, as convictive, as it is consistent with moral probability to obtain, until time, in the course of his revolutions, shall develope, those mysteries, which are yet obsured from general knowledge, and only committed in mutual confidence to the principal performers.

When a survey was made of the stores in the grand arsenal and store-rooms last year, amongst many, a deficiency appeared, of 21,979 stands of arms, and 40,047 bayonets, the chief part of which, stood on the Store-keeper's books, as *compleat and new*, and as *serviceable*.——As there appeared but from ten, to eleven thousand stands in the grand magazine, where the Company intended that there should never be less than forty thousand, which number, they imagined were then actually in store; a number scarce adequate to the troops entertained by the Presidency of Bengal alone;——So alarming a deficiency, at so critical a period, when all India as well as Europe were in motion, apparently with hostile designs against Britain, it could not fail to excite such an astonishment, as produced an enquiry; when it appeared that without the leave of the Board of Inspection or the Board of Ordnance, and without the concurrence or knowledge of the military Store-keeper, those arms were sent by the Commissary of stores to the public Vendue office, in order to be sold by public out-cry. After having lain many months in a damp cellar, where they must have contracted a sufficient degree of rust, to render the best and highest polished arms in the tower of London, unserviceable; upon a survey, by the military Store-keeper, he found them to his surprize, in the good condition (notwithstanding the humid air and total neglect of them for so long a time) which he represented in a letter, written officially, but tenderly, to the Board of Ordnance, of which the following is a literal abstract.

"November 27, 1779. I beg leave further to sub-
"mit another observation to the Board, that the
"21,979 stand of arms, and 40,047 bayonets, ap-
"peared on the survey not to have been in so bad a
"state as I had at first apprehended; the militia were
"since supplied from them, and in my opinion, many
"more may be made fit for service, *as there is an estab-
"lishment in this department for repairing them.* If it
"were the pleasure of the Board, I would recommend
"it to them to appoint three or four military gentlemen

" men of the Ordnance department, or other mili-
" tary officers, high in station, to review them, be-
" fore they are exposed to sale, as I would not chuse to
" take upon myself to condemn so large a quantity of
" valuable arms, from my own observation. At all
" events the opinion of competent judges, can be had
" at this time at the presidency; I could even wish
" the final orders regarding them were submitted to
" the Governor and Council, *some of the arms standing*
" *upon the books of this department as compleat and new.*
" *Another reason which induces me to recommend this to*
" *the attention of the Board, is, the consideration that*
" *there are only* 10 *or* 11,000 *serviceable arms in the*
" *grand magazine, and that* 40,000, *have been always*
" *deemed the proper and necessary establishment in store,*
" *for the defence of Bengal on emergency.*"

A deficiency of 3503 cartouch-boxes, which the Store-keeper was commanded to *write off* in his books, as if regularly expended on service, together with his refusal to comply, originated the fortunate idea of a general survey, and that it should be continued annually.

Previous to the second annual survey, January 5th, 1780, in consequence of an order from the Board of Inspection to the Board of Ordnance, two questions were sent in circulation to the members of the latter Board, reviving the controversy concerning the additional lock and key of the Store-keeper on each seperate store-room, while that particular room was under examination, and instantly when it's contents were surveyed, the Store-keeper's lock and key to be taken off, and left in the sole charge of the Commissary. " Whether this be adopted as a standing regulation,
" with

" with respect to all future surveys? And whether
" it shall extend to the surveys of all subordinate
" magazines?"

Colonel Watson, in a minute annexed, seemed to have ridiculed the whole proceeding, having observed (doubtless) ironically, " *That he did not understand for*
" *what reason the order was given, as he was of opinion*
" *that the Lieutenant Colonel Green only, can be made*
" *answerable for deficiencies, in future, the Store-keeper*
" *being nominal only.*"

Mr. Wheler maintained his original principle on the subject; said, " That a Store-keeper without his key,
" is a contradiction in terms, and that he will venture
" to affirm, is not to be met with in any other service
" than this; therefore, he moved that the military
" Store-keeper's key, be not only affixed to each
" apartment, during the survey, but that it do like-
" wise continue affixed to the same, when the survey
" of the stores shall be compleated; by which means
" the Store-keeper will become answerable with the
" Commissary, for the property committed to their
" charge."

Mr. Francis concurred with Mr. Wheeler; and Mr. Livius added six constitutional, and indeed incontrovertable reasons to support his concurring opinion.

A circumstance which belongs more properly to another place, is nevertheless obtruded now, by the connection it holds with the subject under censure, as a strong corroborating evidence of the dangerous views of the chief administration in India.

At a time when the Company's territories were threatned with foes and invasion, internal and external; at a time when their arsenals were almost empty; and at a time when œconemy was essential to preserve their credit, even in India, did they expend 57,000 Rupees in the kentledge of the Royal Charlotte,* and that kentledge consisted in military and Ordnance stores from the arsenals, amongst which were 5859 new musket barrels, although there were not double the number remaining in the grand magazine.† To prove that these were sent on board without authority from any person constitutionally qualified to order it: A reference to the letters from the Council to the military Store-keeper, will yield ample satisfaction; of which the following are true copies.

" *Council-Chamber*, 28th *January*, 1780.

To Mr. George Livius, Military Store-keeper.

" Sir,
" It appearing from the books of the Ordnance
" department, that 5859 *Serviceable* musket barrels
" have been sent on board the ship, Royal Charlotte,
" to serve as *kentledge*. I am directed by the Honorable
the

---

* The Resolution also, was at the same time balasted with Balasore pig iron, of the value of 22,000 rupees, by immediate purchase with ready money.

† Why did they not send, as kentledge, the *irreparable* arms in the Vendue office? But that would not answer the intended end. The Indian powers, at enmity with the Company, wanted European arms, and they had their agents at Calcutta. And arms *repaired*, might be *resold* to the Company at high country prices, although bought for a mere trifle at public auction.

"the Governor General and Council, *to call upon you,* *to assign your reasons for having delivered such muskets for the purpose of kentledge;* and to inform the Board, whether all or any part of them have been delivered back into store".

"I am Sir,
"Your most obedient servant.
(Signed) " J. P. Auriol, Secretary."

In answer, Mr. Livius lays before the Board a detail of facts, consistent with the station to which he was *reduced,* and a seasonable rebuke for the inconsistent application for information, to a Store-keeper whom that Board has deliberately stripped of the prerogatives of his office, as their application, according to their own regulations, should have been *solely* directed to Colonel Green, the Commissary of Stores, and the *effectual* Store-keeper.

" *Fort-William,* 29th *January,* 1780.
" To J. P. Auriol, Esquire, Secretary."

" Sir, I have received your letter of yesterday's date. I received no order from the Board of Ordnance to issue the 5859 serviceable musket barrels, *which you inform me,* were sent on board the ship Royal Charlotte; nor does the Ordnance department *(by positive orders from the Governor General and Council and by the Ordnance standing regulations)* issue any *but by indent of the Store-keeper.* It is therefore out of my power to assign reasons, *(for which you called upon me)* for having delivered such musket barrels for the purpose of kentledge; *they were issued without my knowledge.* In reply to your second requisition, whether any part have been delivered back into store, I do myself the
" honor

"honor to inclose a copy of the indent of stores re-
"turned from the Master Attendant, *this day*, which
"are all that I have any account of.
"I am, Sir,
"Your most obedient servant.
(Signed) "G. Livius, M. S. K.

Mr. Livius that day received from Mr. John Petrie, acting Marine Paymaster, the letter which is referred to in the above answer to Mr. Secretary Auriol, viz.

To George Livius, Esquire, M. S. K.
"Sir,
"You will please to order to be received into the
"honourable Company's arsenal, the following iron
"kentledge, *which remain on board the ships Royal Char-
"lotte and Resolution.**

"On board thee Royal Charlotte.
"Musket barrels, *serviceable*   5859 ⎱ 11,922
"Ditto,   -   - *unserviceable* 6063 ⎰
"Ordnance iron guns, *ditto*,   -   -   176
"Country iron shot, *serviceable*, -   -   4053
"Ditto, *unserviceable*,   -   -   -   7313
"Some pig iron.
"On board the Resolution.
"A quantity of small iron kentledge.
"I am, Sir,
"Your most obedient servant.
"Marine Pay-office (signed) J. Petrie, A. M. P. M.
"29th January, 1780."

This

---

* The Royal Charlotte was laid up on the 21st of the preceding August, and serviceable arms continued on board. The return is an exact copy of the indent, by which it was originally received on board from the marine department.

This tranfaction is fo diftinct, that it needs no comment, but that it is prefumable, that *ferviceable* mufket barrels, ftowed as kentledge in a fhip's hold, from July, 1778, to February, 1780, muft have been rendered *unferviceable*; and that in all probability, they, and the other ftores, would have remained on board, without thought or care, and be fold with the fhips, had not the matter been happily fuggefted to a member of Council, who, until then, was a ftranger to the whole clandeftine management and abufe.

Under fuch perplexing and injurious predicaments, with a deliberate defign, (open to the licenced rapacity of fuch as conceive upon a fixed principle of faith, which is become proverbial in that fettlement, that no plunder or peculation from the Company is difhoneft or unjuft, and that no action can be offenfive or criminal, while the actors are favoured by a majority of Government) is not only the Company's property expofed, but the very fafety and exiftence of their poffeffions and trade, ftaked, to humour the caprice of fome principal fervants, and to enrich themfelves and their partizans, in Bengal. It is therefore incumbent upon the Directors, as a diftinguifhing proof of fidelity to their conftituents, and loyalty to their country, either to enforce their orders, and affert their legal authority, with manly fpirit, or to fink under the influence of corruption, and yield up their mock-power to the minifters of their own creation abroad; taking fpecial care, in order to be confiftent throughout, to difmifs from their fervice, as unworthy of *public* confidence, thofe, whofe *private* virtues, have dared to be *publickly* honeft, and who, with becoming deference, have endeavoured by indefatigable affiduity and unremitting pains, to maintain the authority of the Company, and the dignity and honor of the Britifh nation in Hindoftan.

FINIS.

www.ingramcontent.com/pod-product-compliance
Lightning Source LLC
Chambersburg PA
CBHW021803230426
43669CB00008B/620